Growing Up BLACK in WHITE

KEVIN D. HOFMANN

ISBN: 1543050913
ISBN-13: 9781543050912

God is the reason this book was made possible. As I complete this second edition, I would like to rededicate this book to God, who chose me to live out such an interesting life.

I would also like to dedicate this book to my parents. The sacrifices you made for me are humbling.

Lastly, I would like to dedicate this book to my wife, Shilease, and two sons, Tai and Zion. Thanks for giving up quality time, so I could retrace my life and do the work I was created to do.

TABLE OF CONTENTS

FOREWORD

What a unique way to grow up. Our family was part of the second wave of multicultural families created through transracial adoption in the late sixties. We had no role models to help guide us through this interesting life. This book recounts our uncharted journey, and I added the last chapter to give today's families what my family didn't have. Chapter twenty-three is a map to help families get the things right that we struggled with as a multicultural family. I hope you enjoy our journey and learn from it. More importantly I hope you will use the twenty third chapter to fashion a family that raises amazing children confident in who they are and where they come from.

1

WELCOME

The flames shoot skyward and claw at the moon. The orange and yellow tongues of fire dance above the shades of blue. I am still sound asleep in my crib, enjoying the last moments of blessed peace. At eleven months old, I am cocooned in the land of dreams and unwilling to leave.

It's the summer of 1968, and these flames are coming from the front yard of our Monroe Street home in Dearborn, Michigan, a small suburb of Detroit. The sound of voices on the front lawn in the early summer morning hours brings Mom and Dad out of their restful sleep. Mom springs out of bed when she sees the reflections of the flames on the ceiling and walls of her second-story bedroom. At the window she only sees a blurry glow of fire below. She doesn't take the time to get her glasses, so her vision is limited to shadows and flickering lights. Her mind recognizes it as fire, but her nearsighted eyes can't focus enough to tell what is on fire.

My three siblings join me in undisturbed sleep, each in our own beds across the hall. The mother instincts tears at her chest. She is conflicted between running to the phone to call for help and running to her four children to protect them. The phone is downstairs, and her children are upstairs. Instead, Mom dispatches Dad to check on us while she races to the phone.

As Mom exits her room, she grabs her glasses, purposely dodging the windows in case the voices are looking for a human target. As she goes down the stairs and turns to the right, she hurries into the den and picks up the heavy Bell telephone and dials zero.

The answer to the question that is racing around in her head still has not come: What is on fire? Putting together thoughts is nearly impossible. Panic and fear whirl inside her head. Mom wants to cry and scream for help, but no one but the perpetrators will hear her.

The trip down the stairs brings her closer to the fire, and it seems to be right outside the window and moving quickly toward the house. The bright shadows and confusion tell a convincing story. As Mom is waiting for the help on the other end of the phone to pick up, she becomes certain the fire is consuming the wooden plantation-style porch. Soon the fire will find its way into the house, and the owners of the voices may not be too far behind.

The operator picks up the phone, and Mom pleads for help, desperately wishing they could send the help through the phone lines. Instead, the emotionless operator assures her help is on the way. As Mom returns the phone to the cradle, she prays the operator will respect the panic in her voice and send help right away.

Climbing back up the stairs to Dad and the kids, Mom is relieved to move away from the fire and invisible voices. Dad meets Mom at the top of the steps. Relief washes over Mom when she hears that all four kids are asleep and have no knowledge of the front-yard fireworks. The pace of the morning chaos slows down considerably with Dad's report.

Mom and Dad return to their room to get a better view of the fire below. Their aerial perspective brings a harsh clarity to the situation. The fire comes from a six-foot cross in the middle of their spacious front lawn. The flames simmer, and the crackle of burning wood is all that can be heard. The voices have disappeared, leaving their glowing calling card.

The apartment building next door begins to awaken. The dark windows of the apartments begin to flash one by one against the night backdrop. As each light pops on, the feeling of isolation is driven further away.

Another flash appears as the exterior door to the apartment building is pushed open. The bright light across the dark yard outlines the silhouette of a young man. He marches quickly and with purpose to the burning cross, which has burned down to coal. The march pours into a jog and then a run—as he zeros in on his target, he leaps feet first into the cross. His perfectly targeted kick to its base knocks it to the ground. The impact forces glowing wood and sparks to jump into the air. The young man turns sharply and walks back into the light from the open door. He slams the door behind him, and the street is now early-morning quiet again.

After forty-five minutes, the Dearborn police arrive. They ask the necessary questions to complete their report, and then they leave. Mom and Dad are not comforted by their presence, nor are they convinced any investigation will occur beyond the paper report.

As the sun rises on the charred and broken cross, my parents replay the last eight months of candid feedback and disapproving glances from neighbors. It doesn't take them long to wonder who initiated the visit, even if the neighbors weren't actually the ones to strike the match.

What Mom and Dad have done has shaken up their small community, and the community is now shaking them back. In November of 1967, my parents brought me home for the first time. I traveled from a foster home in the neighboring city of Detroit to the parsonage occupied by Mom, Dad, and their three children. Dad was a white associate pastor at the nearby all-white Lutheran church. Mom was a busy homemaker who attended to three children five years old and younger. Now added to the mix was me, a three-month-old biracial child. My white biological mother and black biological father had combined to create a child with skin the color of a toasted marshmallow. My presence in that house started a controversy no one would have predicted.

Throughout my childhood, my adoptive parents, being a pastor and the wife of a pastor, strive to live what their Christian faith taught them: When someone is in need, you help him. When someone needs a helping hand, you offer yours. Unfortunately, Dearborn is not a city of pastors, and we will soon learn not all pastors and/or Christians are eager to extend their hands.

I laugh today when I see large wooden animals in a neighbor's yard that have been erected to celebrate an important event.

They usually have a catchy sign attached that says something like, "Lordy, Lordy, Cathy's forty," or, "Oh joy, it's a boy." This is a way for people to acknowledge and publicly celebrate something. Then I think back to the wooden welcome I got in Dearborn.

It is usually easy to select a gift when someone has a baby. You bring diapers, a sippy cup and plate set, or maybe a playpen. When people get married, it's even easier. They have a list to pick from at a local store. The dilemma comes when a white family, in one of the whitest cities in America during the Civil Rights Movement, brings home a biracial child. What do you do to make an eleven-month-old biracial boy feel welcome?

A flaming cross seems like the perfect way to say, "Welcome to Dearborn."

To understand why and how an irrational fear sounds so rational to so many, you have to realize what is going on in 1968 in Southeast Michigan. You have to go back twelve months to the summer of 1967.

In the summer of 1967, Detroit is diagnosed with an inoperable cancer three weeks before I take my first breath. In the early-morning hours of July 23, 1967, the city's disease can no longer contain itself. What begins as a celebration rages into a full-blown insurrection that is recorded on national TV.

At the corner of Twelfth Street and Clairmont on Detroit's northwest side (a predominately black neighborhood), several gather on this Saturday night and early Sunday morning to celebrate two Vietnam vets returning home from the war. The welcome-home party takes place in an illegal after-hours club.

As the alcohol is poured and glasses are raised to toast the heroes, Motown music shares the air with cigarette smoke and oxygen. Martha Reeves and the Vandellas ask when Jimmy Mack is coming back. Their question floats on the dense air. Marvin Gay and Tammi Terrell sing back and forth about a love that can't be contained by a mountain, no matter how high. And the Four Tops harmonize about sweet Bernadette.

At about 3:30 a.m. on Sunday morning, the Detroit Police Department, which is mostly white, joins the party. Their plan is to raid the after-hours club and arrest the patrons inside. The first police on the scene find more partygoers than they expect, so they call for additional support and wait. While they wait for backup, a crowd begins to gather from the neighborhood. The tension begins to swell in this black community; years and years of mistreatment by whites, lack of opportunity, and disrespect have pushed the community closer and closer to its boiling point. On this early morning the blacks in Detroit will voice in unison that they have had enough.

The sweet sounds of Motown are replaced with angry chants and the ping of breaking glass. Fires crackle, and the suffocating smell of burning buildings and furniture replace the recent smell of alcohol. Within hours, the destruction consumes the neighborhood and spills over into the surrounding neighborhoods as the angry crowds grow.

People watch helplessly as the fires greedily eat up property in neighborhoods deemed too dangerous for the fire department to enter.

Soon the National Guard arrives to help control the unrest. They march down the streets of Detroit with weapons at their sides, escorted by armed tanks. They are dressed for war in the middle of a city, and Detroit quickly transforms into a war zone. The presence of the National Guard only adds fuel to an already uncontrollable fire.

After five long days Detroit lies quiet and smoldering. It's been opened from chin to navel, and there exposed on national TV is a massive tumor that has been growing untreated for decades.

Two and a half weeks after the raid at Twelfth Street, in Martin Place West Hospital, I am born. I emerge from my white mother, put there by my black father in a time where different pigments can't get along. Fortunately for me, hormones trump pigment.

Thirty-five years after this series of events unfolds, I sit down with Mom and Dad, and they share with me their early memories of my life with them. For the first time I hear the fiery-cross story, and I am humbled.

Being adopted brings with it the special feeling of being specifically chosen by your adoptive family. Throughout my life, that special feeling walked hand in hand with the guilt that I felt for being the cause of such turmoil.

Being a parent by definition means sacrifice, but what my parents endured was Herculean. I often reflect back at this scene and that time, and I marvel at the couple who chose to bring color to a city that did not want to be colorized. I marvel at their courage to do what was right when all around them told them it was wrong.

My birth occurred in the middle of this racial hurricane. In my veins flow black and white, created in a time when the lines were boldly outlined, and no one was to cross them, yet my birth parents ignored those lines and created me. Again, I am humbled, but at the same time I feel so very special.

It is my belief that each adoptee is divinely matched and placed with his or her adoptive family. As my parents continued to tell me the story of how I arrived in their care, this belief was confirmed. As they welcomed me in to their home, I beat odds no Las Vegas bookie would ever bet on.

2

GOD ODDS

The odds of eating an oyster and finding a pearl—1 in 12,000.
The odds of being struck by lightning—1 in 200,000.
The odds of getting pregnant with quadruplets—1 in 705,000.

What are the odds of a biracial baby up for adoption in Detroit getting placed in a permanent home in 1967?

In early 1967, a Lutheran minister, Pastor Hofmann, and his wife set out to complete their family. They have been blessed with three healthy children to this point, but the physical toll on the wife after the third pregnancy means the fourth child will have to come by way of adoption.

The pastor and his wife contact a private adoption agency to complete their family plan. In early 1967 the couple begins the climb up and over the mountain of paperwork, the thorough background checks, and the necessary home visits. One by one the required items are scratched off the list, and the couple is approved for adoption.

Then they wait.

The 1967 tulips bloom and die. The late-spring winds blow through the large trees on Monroe Street. The summer grass comes in, creating a natural carpet for children to play. Teenage boys walk behind push mowers. Then baseball games start and end as August passes. Rakes replace the mowers, and the same able-bodied homeowners exchange aching lawn-mowing muscles for aching raking muscles.

And still the couple waits for their baby.

The sun comes out less and less. A riot begins and ends six miles away, and a city is changed forever. It is close enough to be scary, but in 1967, six miles to Detroit is a lifetime away.

The phone in the Hofmann household sits quiet.

In the summer of 1967, I am born. My mother places me with a private Lutheran adoption agency rather than with the state. Twenty-one years later, I find out my birth mother has no connection with the Lutheran faith, but this choice on her part substantially raised my chances of finding a permanent home.

My placement with a private agency versus the state means the odds of my placement into a permanent home get substantially better. I am placed in a foster home on the west side of Detroit, in the care of my foster mother, Mrs. Curry, a gentle and caring black woman in her sixties. She is married, and she and Mr. Curry name me David and give me my first home.

As I settle into my new home, Mrs. Hofmann, the wife of Pastor Hofmann, dials the number to the adoption agency located in downtown Detroit. Mrs. Hofmann has grown tired of all the waiting with no answers. She is put in touch with the director, who explains that the right child has not come along yet. The director explains that since the couple has qualified for a "hard to place" child, the search isn't as easy. This is the first time Mrs. Hofmann has heard the phrase "hard to place child," so the young mother asks what that means exactly. It is explained that since the couple already has their own children, they will have to accept a child who is harder to place.

The director explains that she does have a child who qualifies, if they are interested. The child is a baby girl who was born with a heart defect, a hole in the heart. The director goes on to explain that this special-needs child will need extensive medical attention for many years and that there is no guarantee the child will survive.

The couple thinks it over for a few days. They consider the attention, the emotional expense, and the financial expense. The care for this child will be very taxing to all areas. They already have three children, and on a pastor's salary, there is not a lot of extra room. All the medical expenses for their children to date are taken care of by a charitable pediatrician who understands the wallet size of a preacher. This little girl is simply a mountain the Hofmanns can't climb.

They call the director to explain the little girl is not a challenge they are able to take on. The director understands and inquires if they would be interested in a different kind of "hard to place" child.

The races in the late sixties in Detroit are so polarized that neither race wants a child with part of the other's race. The whites want a white child, and the blacks want a black child; therefore a biracial child in Detroit, Michigan, in 1967 qualifies as "hard to place."

To even pose this question is a risk, but the director has to lob it out there to see if they will swing at it. For her, it is a safe risk. This is a Christian family, after all—how can they object?

Her gamble pays off. The couple graciously agrees to put "biracial" on their list. The director goes back to work to find the right child, and the waiting begins again.

The postman brings hope sealed in an invitation delivered one day in November. The invitation comes from the adoption agency. They are having a tea at their main office on West Grand Boulevard in Detroit. The tea is designed to bring together potential parents, potential foster parents, current foster parents, and children up for adoption. It is created to spark interest in becoming foster parents, to hopefully match up parents with adoptees, and to show what services the agency has to offer. The Hofmanns put the date on their calendar and plan to attend.

The coveted date arrives, and they make their way to the main office of the adoption agency. Inside there is a large room with rows and rows of folding chairs that take over the middle of the room. People speak politely in the way most people do when they are nervous and unsure what else to do. It is easy to tell the potential parents from the foster parents. There is energy in the eyes of the potential parents. There is a special way their smiles curl. The Hofmanns have that look.

As the small groups break up and everyone takes their seats, The agency begins to circulate the foster children around the room. The hopeful parents handle, admire, and burp children like they are containers at a Tupperware party.

That day my foster mother, Mrs. Curry, exits her home shortly after she dresses me for the cool Detroit November air. I arrive in the room, and Mrs. Curry knows the drill. She has been a foster mother for many years, and I am sure she has been to plenty of teas. She surrenders me shortly after entering the room and sends me on my journey. I too am passed from one set of waiting arms to another. As I land in the arms of Mrs. Hofmann, the director of the agency strolls by and remarks, "This would be the perfect baby for you if he were only a girl." Distracted by the excitement of our first meeting, the Hofmanns don't process what the director has said. They hold me for a few moments and then politely send me on my way down the row.

I continue on my publicity junket as Mr. and Mrs. Hofmann process the comment the director made. The confused hopeful parents turn to each other and ask the same question: "Who told her we were only interested in a girl?"

As the tea concludes, the Hofmanns approach the director and ask where she got the idea that they only wanted a girl. She admits that she innocently and independently thought that, since they already had two boys and one girl, they needed another girl to make the family symmetrical.

Humbly the Hofmanns explain they would be interested in adding another boy to their family. In particular, they are interested in the child who the director thought would be perfect for them, even if he is a boy. The Hofmanns formally inquire about making me a part of their family. The director schedules an appointment to sit down and discuss the possibilities of adopting me.

The date of the scheduled appointment comes, and the Hofmanns arrive to discuss the next step in the process. They sit at the director's desk and are informed that I am available for adoption. The director only has to verify if I have had a recent trip to the pediatrician. It is standard procedure to confirm the health of the child before the adoption can move forward. The director calls my caseworker as the Hofmanns sit waiting for the news. Although they can only hear one end of the conversation, it is evident by the tone of the, "Oh, yes, I see," that the response to her question isn't positive. When she hangs up the phone, she confirms I have not recently been seen by a pediatrician. In fact, my last medical evaluation was three months ago during my short stay at Martin Place West Hospital when I was born.

The Hofmanns sit at the desk, disappointed, not knowing if this will mean months and months of red tape. It could mean months of worrying about my health and whether I will also need extensive care. This answer could mean so many possibilities— too many possibilities.

"Why don't you go pick him up from the foster home and have him looked at by your pediatrician? If the doctor checks out, you can keep him," the director says.

"What if there is something wrong with him?" asks Mrs. Hofmann.

"Just bring him back." This reply comes back without a pause. "Just take him home and try him out. If he doesn't work out, just bring him back," the director encourages. She does not see the absurdity in her comments. She is just anxious to close a deal that isn't expected to get closed.

The offer that is presented doesn't sit level. The generosity in the offer tilts the scales toward a yes, but the sense that some rule or procedure is being ignored shifts the weight toward uncertainty. The nagging feeling that this deal shouldn't be made in this way causes the Hofmanns to pause.

While they debate the unusual offer, the director pushes the conversation forward. She sees the impossible is actually possible, and she does not want to waste a second for a no to creep in. She pushes the paperwork forward as she places a call to Mrs. Curry. The phone call is quick and concise, just enough time to get the needed information. She returns the phone back to its cradle and advises that Mrs. Curry will have me ready momentarily. The Hofmanns are shuffled out of her office, given directions to Mrs. Curry's residence, and congratulated all in a matter of seconds.

The Hofmanns are halfway to Mrs. Curry's before they realize what has taken place. The signing of papers occurred somewhere in this organized confusion. As they signed the last "n" in "Hofmann" they were transformed from Mr. and Mrs. Hofmann to my mom and dad.

The offer is never contemplated or discussed. The Hofmanns decide separately and silently once they pick me up that I will be permanently placed—in their family.

They pull up to Mrs. Curry's home on Birwood Street. As promised, Mrs. Curry has me packed and ready to go. My foster mother is soft spoken, respectful, and kind as she gently hands me over. The bewildered new parents reach for me, and Mrs. Curry's reassuring smile passes to them hope, the kind of hope that assures them everything will be OK.

The odds of a biracial child up for adoption being placed in a permanent home in Detroit in 1967—insurmountable. The odds of this union coming together are God odds, odds only God can overcome. On that November afternoon, God places me in the arms of the family that he chooses just for me. But getting others to agree on God's placement will also be insurmountable.

3

HEARTBROKEN

Eight years before I am placed in Mom and Dad's arms, Grandpa grabs the phone as it rings in their Grosse Pointe, Michigan, home. On the other end of the phone is the night-shift supervisor at the Budd Company plant in Detroit. Grandpa has gained a reputation of being able to handle "them," and this time "they" are out of control. The "they" and "them" are the blacks who work on the line at Budd. Tonight the line is shut down due to a mechanical problem. Usually when the line is shut down, "they" retreat to the men's bathroom and set up shop while the problem is repaired.

Tonight, constructed in the small washroom is a miniature bar with alcohol and drugs. "They" take the doors off the stalls, lay them on the floor, and use them to shoot dice.

The party reaches its pinnacle just as the horn sounds calling them back to the line. The machine is fixed. When management insists they get back to work, "they" refuse, and it gets back to management that someone may have a gun. Management panics and calls Grandpa to assist.

Grandpa hangs up the phone and heads out the door. He is on his way to see if he can work his magic and get "them" to behave. As he drives into the parking lot, one of the "goodies" (the blacks who behave, but not enough to be considered outside of "they") approaches Grandpa.

"Don't go in there, boss—they might kill you."

Grandpa ignores the warning and marches into the plant and straight into the homemade bar. He jumps up on the urinal and tells "them" to wrap it up, close the bar, and get back to work—and "they" do. Grandpa leaves as quickly as he came and returns home.

He will later tell Grandma he was shaking as he stood on the urinal and shouted. He will admit he came close to leaving a deposit in the urinal he was standing on. Fortunately, Grandpa got the line up and running, proving he knew how to handle "them."

This is the story my grandmother relays to me as I interview her for this book. These are her terms and her account. I am not sure how accurate it is, but it is entertaining. Hearing her tell the story with no apologies, unaware of how offensive her version is, I am entertained. I am entertained by her view of blacks. It sounds like she is telling a story about some wild animals that got loose, and about Grandpa, the animal trainer who was called in to round 'em up—and who did it absent a chair or a whip.

Mom grew up in Philadelphia, Pennsylvania, the daughter of Grandpa, the "animal trainer." In their house there were lines drawn around races, and one race was seen as superior to another. This mentality was handed down to Mom, but Mom chose not to imitate it.

This is seen very clearly in a gift that was given to Mom when she was a young girl. On one special occasion, Mom was given a black doll named Niggy. The origin of the doll or its name Mom couldn't remember, but Niggy was an accepted part of her early childhood.

In this same house, Mom was not allowed to bring home a black friend from school because blacks were not allowed unless they were stuffed and named Niggy—or unless they were Juanita, the "colored" cleaning lady who came once a week.

In this house, referring to blacks as "they" and "them" was OK.

In this house, these were the accepted talk and attitudes of many. They were so a part of Grandma that she never let them go and never saw them as wrong. Even when sharing stories with her biracial grandson.

On November 14, 1967, I am carried across the threshold into my new house. I am three months old and already in my second home. There to greet me are my new brothers and sister, who had no idea I was coming home today. My big sister Lisa and big brothers James and Matthew are there full of grins and smiles. I am placed on the dining-room table in my bassinet like an early Thanksgiving turkey, and all our eyes shine with excitement. We are instant siblings, and they don't even know what to call me. Lisa suggests the name Kevin, after a young boy she was so fond of in elementary school. All agree, and I am given the name Kevin. David, the name given to me by my foster mother, becomes my middle name.

During the excitement of the next few days, Mom's excitement splits time with fear. Her parents are on their way to Dearborn. Mom is concerned with how her old house will receive her new house.

In those quiet hours, Mom and I rock in the black wooden rocking chair that Grandpa made with his own hands. As Mom feeds me, I am sure she is reminded of Niggy, the doll she pretended to feed and rock to sleep many years before. It is a thought that comes back to her often in those first few days.

Grandpa and Grandma's journey to this point has been a busy one. Grandpa was transferred from the foundry with the Budd Company in Philadelphia to the Budd plant in Detroit. After nine years with Budd in Detroit, his fondness for alcohol brought the job to a quick end. From there, Grandpa found a job as a consultant for a foundry in India. He and Grandma moved to India for three years, but his bottle cut that job short too.

Now, their first stop back in the states is in Dearborn to see my mom and dad and the newly expanded family.

The overseas communication has been minimal, so Grandma and Grandpa only know part of the adoption story. They know Mom and Dad are going to adopt a fourth child, but they don't know when, and they are unaware of the "hard to place" twist. They find out just how special I am the second they peer into my bassinet.

At our introduction, I am placed in Grandma's arms, and she stares at me. Shock dissolves what little inhibitions Grandma has, and she quickly asks, "Well, what is he? He looks Indian!"

My fair skin and racial makeup produce what Grandma thinks is a child from India. Fresh from India, Grandma fuses recent memory with my biracial tone. She passes me to Grandpa without saying much else, and he quickly agrees: "Boy, he does look like an Indian baby."

Sitting in Grandma's apartment, Grandma and I reminisce about the thirty-five years of my life leading up to the day of this interview. Grandpa is no longer with us, and in the same manner as she tells Grandpa's plant story, she tells all her stories. No apologies, no concessions. Grandma continues as she proudly tells me the story of my baptism.

It is a few weeks after our first meeting. Grandma and Grandpa are still visiting in Dearborn when Mom and Dad schedule my baptism.

The head pastor of the church does not share Mom and Dad's enthusiasm for diversity. Instead, he refuses to baptize me. He doesn't want to support my presence in the city or in his church in any way. The younger pastor, who is also an assistant with Dad, sees no problem with it and agrees to baptize me. The head pastor reluctantly agrees to allow me to be baptized.

The morning of my baptism, Dad comes back to the house after the first service to say the head pastor has changed his mind. Now he will not allow the baptism at all, no matter who does it. Mom and Dad are surprised but not shocked. The pastor has made it very clear what he thinks of their choice in children.

Dad tells Mom to bring me to the later service ready to be baptized, and Dad returns to church to try and convince his pastor to change his mind.

We arrive at the late service, and the baptism is now on again. Dad has somehow convinced the head pastor to allow my baptism. I am baptized by the younger assistant pastor. Grandma sits in the pew intensely watching Mom as I am being baptized. She can see the redness that flows to Mom's cheeks, the same redness that attacks Mom's face when she eats spicy foods. She can see Mom's jaw contract as she grits her teeth, hoping no one will stand up and oppose the baptism. Fortunately, there isn't an invitation in a baptism to "speak now or forever hold your peace."

As soon as I am baptized, the redness in Mom's cheeks and the tightness in her jaw wash away. Mom carries me back to the pew and places me in Grandma's arms. Throughout the whole service, I don't make a sound, not even when they pour the water on my head. Grandma sits holding the Indian-looking baby, beaming with pride.

The prideful moment doesn't last long. It is interrupted by the noticeable tension that fills the church. Since my introduction to the church, there has been a growing debate between those who support my presence and those that don't. Up until my baptism, those who opposed my inclusion in the church would gather in small circles and discuss why my presence should not be allowed. Those who supported my inclusion would do the same. The two opposing groups never came together until today. The issue that they disagreed about was lying in Mom's arms in front of the church. Anyone scanning the faces in the crowd as I am baptized can easily tell who stands on which side of this debate. After church, Grandma and Grandpa go straight back to our house. They don't stay to socialize over coffee and doughnuts because the tense environment makes Grandma nauseous.

Grandma and Grandpa stay for a few more weeks, and then they leave for Chicago to go spend time with Grandma's sister. They will soon settle in Florida in a house Grandpa will build.

A year later, Grandma and Grandpa return for another visit. They are afraid for their daughter after they hear about the cross-burning incident that took place a few months before.

They worry about the daughter who has four kids all under the age of six to take care of. Grandma is afraid the attacks will become more personal and that someone in her daughter's family might get killed. In the past year, the assassinations of Dr. Martin Luther King and Bobby Kennedy have taken place, so the fear that someone could be killed is very real.

Grandma is simply a mother worrying about the safety of her daughter.

During their visit, Mom returns home from a trip to her hairdresser. She is visibly upset, and her hair is unchanged. Grandma asks what's wrong, and Mom explains through her tears that her hairdresser refused to cut her hair. When Mom asked why, the hairdresser explained it was because she had us kids with her. Mom had been there several times with three out of the four of us, and nothing was ever said. Mom had been there when other customers had their children with them, and nothing was ever said. Embarrassed and furious, Mom left the hairdresser and came home. It was the first and last time I made the trip to that hairdresser.

By now, Mom is used to this type of confrontation, and on any other day, it wouldn't bother her. On this day, she's had enough— enough of the same old thing, enough of the ugliness. It is just enough to make her crack. But there is no better time to crack than when your mother is around. Your mother is there to help cushion your fall during times like these. When Mom finishes her story, she asks in between her sobs, "What am I going to do?"

Grandma's own fears and frustrations over this adoption make it difficult for her to see her crying daughter in front of her. Grandma tries to sort out her own feelings and disregards Mom's feelings.

"Well, what did you expect? What you did was so out of the ordinary," barked Grandma. "What did you expect? You had to expect this kind of reaction, and by the way, what do you think my friends are going to say when they find out what you did?"

Instead of comfort, Mom gets scolded like a child who has done something very wrong.

At first blush, it's hard to follow Grandma's line of thinking. How could she be so cruel? I have to recall what Grandma told me in the interview earlier.

Grandma remembers a day in Detroit many years ago when she and Grandpa were out shopping in the upscale shopping district on Grand River Avenue. As they strolled from store to store enjoying a quiet Sunday afternoon, two black men who worked for Grandpa approached them.

"Hey, how you doing, boss? Good to see you, boss," the men politely stated. Grandpa nodded to the men and continued on down the street. In this tiny moment Grandma was horrified. The white couples with whom they were walking and the whites who passed by all gave Grandma and Grandpa disgusted looks because they were interacting with these black men. Grandma, who envisioned herself a socialite, was devastated by this incident that lasted less than three seconds.

If that exchange mortified Grandma, it is easy to see how having one of "them" in her family would be troubling.

In that conversation with Mom in 1968, I think part of Grandma was thinking, "How could my own daughter do this to me?" Whether her thoughts were justified or not, I have come to understand how deeply Grandma was affected by my adoption.

The true depth of how she was affected comes in one answer during our interview. I ask Grandma how she felt back then about her daughter adopting a biracial baby. I ask the question right after she has told the hairdresser story, and I receive an answer I do not expect.

The emotions of the hairdresser story have taken Grandma back to that place and time. I can tell by the way she sounds, how she tells the story, and by that distant "I am not here look" she gets. It is the purest and most honest answer I get all day. Quietly, Grandma answers, "I was heartbroken."

On my way home from our interview, that answer bounces off the walls of my skull over and over again. As I look back at my childhood, I can never remember an incident when Grandma or Grandpa was harsh or rude to me. I can never remember an incident where their true thoughts bled through their Grandma and Grandpa façades.

However, as I sit behind the wheel contemplating our talk, there is one incident that comes back to me as I scan through years and years of interaction with Grandma and Grandpa. This incident is pulled from my memory in high definition.

Grandma and Grandpa were visiting us in Detroit. They would usually visit about once a year. Mom and Dad, my brothers James and Matthew, and I were picnicking in the park with Grandma and Grandpa. The orange and brown leaves painted in my memory tell me the picnic was sometime in the early fall. The sun was bright and warming, and I was watching James, Matthew, and Grandpa wrestling in a mound of leaves. I was in my late adolescent or early teen years. Lisa, my sister, was not present, and I don't know why. I assume the importance of her teenaged years overruled wanting to spend time with the family.

Watching Grandpa interact with my brothers on this fall day was like watching TV. I was watching it but not a part of it. I wasn't invited in, and I remember feeling left out. They each pitched handfuls of leaves at each other, and James and Matthew ganged up on Grandpa. They were laughing and screaming as the leaves floated in the air. It was a scene Norman Rockwell would have coveted, and I was not in it. I remember seeing their interaction and wondering why Grandpa and I never interacted that way. There was an easiness that their relationship had that ours did not.

This disconnect seemed obvious that day. I didn't feel a bond with them as it appeared my brothers did. Watching them play together showed me a truth I didn't know how to handle: I was kept at a safe distance, and I never made it into that inner circle. At that time, the thought of an adult being wrong or doing wrong was foreign to me, so I concluded that something about me was unapproachable. Something about me caused that gap.

Since it was never what they did, but rather what they didn't do, that separated us, I assumed the responsibility for what I saw as a fracture in our relationship. What they didn't do was treat me like *their* grandchild. Instead I was treated like a friend of the family; it was like my adoption was never finalized.

On my car ride home from my interview with Grandma, I piece together what I learned in the interview and in this very clear picnic scene. The revelation that it was *not* me gives me momentary relief. The feeling of relief is followed with sadness as the gravity of this revelation slams onto the top of my head.

I wonder if that is why Grandma and Grandpa only came around once a year. I wonder if Mom understood her parents and understood limited contact with them was best. I am sure now Mom and Dad saw what I couldn't see and had to answer the difficult question, "What do you do when family won't accept your family?"

This would be the first of a series of difficult questions Mom and Dad would have to contemplate.

The next difficult question they would have to answer was, "What do you do when the church won't accept your family?"

4

THE LUTHERAN INQUISITION

"That's bullshit!" my dad, the associate Lutheran pastor, responds.

A year before God places me in my home on Monroe Street in Dearborn, Mom and Dad are already making waves and losing friends in the church and the community. Living their faith, to them, means acting upon what they studied in church. To Mom and Dad, if all are not treated equally, it is their job to speak up and speak out. One of the ways Mom and Dad do this in 1966 Detroit is by protesting against unfair housing in Southeast Michigan.

Southeast Michigan has had a history of supporting unfair housing practices during the fifties and sixties. It is very difficult for blacks to purchase homes in certain areas. Up until this time, Dearborn has been considered a closed community. Nonwhites are not welcome in Dearborn, and the majority of the residents and the mayor openly support this position.

Mom and Dad feel these types of restrictions are unjust and immoral. They, along with several other people from the Christian community, protest this inequality.

Unfortunately, the church where Dad works doesn't share in Mom and Dad's enthusiasm. Mom and Dad's extracurricular activities are seen by the church as causing problems where there is no problem. The church is made up of a large number of ex-Detroiters who have fled Detroit to get away from the growing black population. Mom and Dad are fighting for the rights of blacks to be able to be live in any neighborhood they choose.

The problem the church sees with this is that it means there is a potential that the neighbors they were trying to get away from in Detroit will follow them to Dearborn. My parents are tinkering with a machine that isn't broken, according to a large majority of the church.

It is comforting to know Mom and Dad were outlaws *before* I arrived.

Mom and Dad know their passion is met with hostility by the church, but they continue to give time to a cause they feel needs their attention. Their ability to see all races as equal helps to explain why adding "biracial" to their list of potential adoptees is an easy choice.

During the height of their protest, my adoption is approved, and I am carried into the church. My presence is the weight that tips the scales. Soon after my introduction to the church, during a staff meeting, the head pastor can no longer control his tongue.

"Did you adopt this boy to make a point and upset the church?" Dad's boss, the "man of God," asks.

"Let me make sure I'm hearing you right. You think we adopted our son to upset the church?" When Dad pauses to clarify the statement, his boss responds with silence.

The pastor sees nothing wrong with what he is implying. But he also knows further explaining himself may dig a hole he is not prepared to climb out of, so he says nothing. At this point, the meeting adjourns before a real argument begins.

The pastor's weak confrontation is a test to see how pliable Dad is. When Dad pushes back, the pastor's strategy changes. His frustration with Dad's actions causes the pastor to step up his attack.

The monthly meetings with the church council now become tense. The church council is the governing body of the local church. The council convenes on a monthly basis to discuss the direction of the church and their presence in the community, finances, and events. Since my arrival, another topic has been added to the meeting schedule. Over and over again, Dad is questioned about his job performance, the way he has done or said something—how he said it, or where he said it, or to whom he said it. Each meeting, the council turns their attention to Dad and reviews what they are unhappy with and how Dad needs to change. It begins subtly, with a simple comment, and over the next few months Dad and his job performance begin to dominate the council meetings.

Finally, Dad is standing on the end of his patience. It is painfully clear what is happening. Instead of pretending it isn't there, Dad walks up to the quiet elephant in the room and asks if this recent concern for his job has anything to do with racism.

Silence floods the room. The "R" word has been uttered, and the council members respond in unison, with an offended tone, that racism has nothing to do with it. They've just noticed that recently *Dad* has changed.

The energy that has been put into avoiding the inevitable confrontation has exhausted the council, and they call for a break.

During the break, Dad, who is still determined to get to the core of the council's issues, approaches a friend and council member.

"OK, what is this really about?" Dad calmly asks his friend.

"They don't think you have the Holy Spirit," replies Dad's friend.

Dad is frozen by the gravity of what has been said. He knows now that since their harassment didn't force him to quit, the council is changing their offensive strategy; they are moving to force him out.

The church bylaws state that although the council has the power to terminate a pastor, they have to base it on something. Dad knows that to fire him, the council has to prove he qualifies for one of the following: he is a heretic, he is immoral, he is mentally incompetent, or he is lazy.

To accuse him of being without the Holy Spirit is a way of saying he is an unbeliever or an immoral person. They not only have the power to terminate him, but if they can fire him by proving he is an unbeliever, they can also make it very difficult for Dad to get work. Who is going to hire a Christian pastor who doesn't believe in God?

In an instant, Dad can see the council trying to grab from him his ability to make a living. In that moment, he sheds his clerical collar for his father's overalls. The rage and fear come alive in his chest and fight their way out. From his lungs to his throat and past his tongue, rage kicks open his lips, and Dad responds, *"That's bullshit!"*

The sound of the trap rings loudly as Dad steps into it. In that moment of panic, he gives the council what they are looking for. What kind of pastor uses words like that? Only an immoral pastor speaks like this.

It is a weak argument, but one that is worth pursuing, the council believes. To present a more convincing case, the council goes to work looking for another straw to grasp. They find it in something Dad shared with the council in an earlier meeting. Dad presented an idea that he found in the Bible. The early church in the Bible would meet in each other's homes and have what has become known as cell church groups. Although this practice is Biblically based and supported, the council finds fault with it. Their response is that this is an act of heresy. Only the communists meet in cell groups. Pastor Hofmann is a heretic.

In this day and time, communism spreading through the United States is a huge concern. If spun right, this provides a great way to get rid of a pastor.

Snap! goes the trap.

Now the council must act. They have an immoral heretic living among them, and he must be extracted.

The next step in terminating a pastor is to call a meeting of the church members and openly charge the pastor. The church then votes on whether to pass a motion to terminate the pastor. The council moves at the speed of sound, and the meeting is put on the church schedule. The acting bishop is called and must preside over the meeting.

One Sunday in the middle of the afternoon, the meeting begins. It is standing room only as over six hundred people attend the meeting. Several community people who know Dad and Mom attend to give their support, but the majority of people are here to see the end of Dad's career. The chance to view a public flogging generates more interest than a Christmas or Easter service.

The meeting is called to order, and the charges are presented. One member after another gets up and tells why they feel Dad is not fit to be a pastor. Dad sits at the front of the church, not able to respond to his accusers. Point after point is made.

"He's a communist."

"He is immoral."

"He lacks the Holy Spirit."

Anyone is free to stand up and say whatever is on his or her mind, and Dad can't debate him or her.

Those who agree with what Dad is trying to do say nothing. They know to speak up in support would mean grave consequences for them in the community, and that could affect *their* jobs or families. Silence brings security.

Punch after punch is thrown, and Dad absorbs them—to the gut, to the jaw, to the head—and he stands defenseless. This torture goes on for three hours, and it is obvious certain people are given scripted things to say.

The wording and timing of each comment is orchestrated. As Dad stands against the ropes, barely able to breathe, the council member who is no longer Dad's friend stands to speak. His role is to tap the last nail into Dad's coffin.

"Pastor Hofmann is immoral!" the council member says loudly. "He...he said..." He pauses, as if unsure if he can say "bullshit" in church, and then bravely continues, "He...said... 'bullshit'!"

The church is still. The whispering chorus that has filled the sanctuary for the last three hours stops.

A snicker cracks the silence. A chuckle escapes out of another member. Slowly, as the church digests what has been said, the laughs join more laughs and rise to the church ceiling, bouncing back and forth.

A grown man just stood up in front of six hundred people to tattle on another grown man for saying a naughty word.

Dad laughs at first, but then embarrassment rises in him. He is embarrassed that he has let his temper put him in this position. Dad knows this was not the way a pastor should act.

As the laughs continue and the tension of the day is finally broken, Dad motions the bishop over for a sidebar. "Maybe I should just resign," he says.

Looking back at Dad, the bishop quietly responds, "Not here, not now." The bishop slowly returns to his seat.

The church is quiet. The inquisition rests. All eyes shift to the bishop.

He rises to address the congregation. Standard procedure says he must now call for a vote. It is no secret. Once it's put to a vote, we will lose. The majority of our supporters are not members of our church. Our supporters come from other churches, so they don't get to cast a vote.

The bishop calmly and decisively changes our future. He begins with a recommendation. The kind of recommendation a parent often gives a child—a recommendation that leaves no room for discussion.

The bishop urges the church to go back to their small committees and talk—talk about the elephant that is roaming the aisles of the church.

"I urge you to discuss the real issues that were raised in this meeting." He quietly puts the issues on the table, the issues that everyone has spent the last three hours ignoring. Then he is done. He never puts it to a vote, and no one openly objects.

We remain at the church for another three years with the bishop's support. The council meetings revert to being more about the church and less about Dad. Life is more tolerable for a season.

Dad and Mom still endure constant insensitive remarks from church members, but by now Mom and Dad have generated thick skin to insulate them from such ignorance. They grow to accept that the mothers in the church nursery refer to me as the "snotty-nosed black kid." Mom and Dad learn to tolerate the obsession that many have that, when I grow up, I might date their daughters. Over and over again, Mom and Dad are approached by concerned parents who ask, "Who do you think he will date when he grows up?"

I can't even pee standing up at this point, but several people are very interested in where my penis will end up.

Mom and Dad turn the other cheek. When Mom takes the kids to the local department store to get pictures, and the photographer asks if Mom wants the "welfare baby" in the pictures, we never get the picture taken.

Mom and Dad stay to help create change, but after three long years they wonder if this constant pressure will change them. They have no other cheeks to offer.

Grandma's words resonate, as a tough decision must now be made. "What did you expect? What you did was so out of the ordinary." Grandma was right. The decision Mom and Dad made to adopt me was extraordinary, not in a heroic sort of way, but in an "out of the ordinary" way. This one decision ushers in the need to make more decisions that are extraordinary, not in a heroic sort of way, but in an "out of the ordinary" way. The decision to leave the white community of Dearborn and move to Detroit into a black community is an extraordinary one—to move into a community where I can be around people like me. The hope is that the new community will be more open to our colorful family.

Dad accepts a call to a church on the northwest side of Detroit. The church has a racially diverse congregation. The parsonage is located a few miles from the church, in a neighborhood that is more black than white and the polar opposite of the Dearborn neighborhood.

This extraordinary decision is made mainly for the benefit of one, and now the rest of the family will experience life as minorities.

5

IDENTITY

The six of us move into a small, three-bedroom, one-story home on Whitcomb Street on the northwest side of Detroit. We move in as the whites continue to pour out to the suburbs.

The church is a beautiful church. I often go into the sanctuary when no one else is there and Dad is back in his office working. The sanctuary is large, and the rows and rows of pews are divided down the middle by a center aisle. The side aisles are both lined with large stained glass windows. In the middle of the day, I like to stroll down the center aisle as the sun illuminates the stained glass windows. The sun casts a colorful shadow across the pews and down on to the floor. The church is quiet and calm and peaceful. It is exactly how church should be.

The reception we receive from the church body is a warm one. This is not to say there aren't those who object to our family composition—they just aren't as open about it as the Dearborn group.

The racial tension in this mixed congregation is there, and the church members struggle with accepting each other. This is a congregation that is quickly changing from white to black, and the older whites struggle with losing "their" church.

Dad has to step up several times to counsel one of the prominent whites in the church. Dad explains calmly and patiently that it is improper to refer to blacks as "them people," especially in church meetings.

The neighborhood is a bigger challenge for our family. The three white kids in our family are the minority in the neighborhood. They don't receive the acceptance that I do. All the kids in our immediate area are black, and they do a good job of making my siblings feel different.

Tony Herb lives directly across the street. He is the oldest of the kids and the leader of the neighborhood. He immediately adopts me as his little brother and calls me his "li'l nigger." It is a term he uses affectionately, and I wear it with honor. Tony is the first friend I remember having. He is about six years older than me and my first role model. I want to be and act just like him. I am in awe of how he responds to every situation. He has a detachment from everything. Tony never lets anything affect him, and his impenetrable swagger is something I covet. He is cool personified, and the fact that he takes a liking to me makes me feel ten feet tall. Tony is the first to plant the seeds of my racial identity. He defines what black is to me.

Two doors down from us is the Davis family, including Marcus, who is a few years older than me, and his two younger sisters. Soon after they moved in, their father left the family, and his amazingly large porn collection, behind. The boys in the neighborhood spend hours admiring the "art." I join them because I don't want to be left out. My conscience tells me what we are doing isn't right, but my desire to be a part of this group is more powerful than doing what is right. Marcus's mother works more than she is home, and the babysitter struggles to keep up with us.

Fred Parker lives a block down, and he is the gregarious chubby kid who has no middle name. Fred is also a few years older than me. The fact that he is missing a middle name strikes us as strange, so we decide to give him one. His middle name will be Puttintang. Its origin comes from the children's rhyme, "Puttintang's my name. Ask me again, I'll tell you the same."

Marcus and Fred teach me the art of the five-fingered discount at the local party store when I am seven. We make the trek to the store daily to purchase Mrs. Davis's king-sized Kools cigarettes. I am too scared to try the five-fingered discount, and they make fun of me because I will not join them. My desire to do wrong has its limits. They are tough kids who seem drawn in by the street life. They too have a swagger, but it is miniature compared to Tony's. I still study them and imitate things about them too.

Marcus and Fred help water the racial-identity seed that Tony has planted.

We live next door to Sonya, who is my age. She lives with her grandparents, mother, and her mother's older brother, who is about fifteen to twenty years older than us. Sonya's father is never spoken of, and I have never seen him. Her uncle comes and goes. He is there for a period, and then he disappears for a time. At five, I wonder why someone so old still lives at home with his parents. He doesn't have a name; he is "Sonya's uncle." He isn't around enough to warrant a name.

Sonya is my first girlfriend, and I am attracted to her chocolate-colored skin. When I am not running after Tony, Marcus, or Fred, I am with Sonya, playing house or making mud pies. My friends tease me about my friendship with Sonya, but as we get older, I learn from my friends that friendships with girls are cool things to have.

One bright summer day, I am playing with Sonya in her backyard, making our famous mud pies. My back is to her screened-in porch, and I am busy pulling the twigs out of the mud pies to make them edible. Behind me I hear a strange noise. As I attempt to swing my body around to see what it is, I am knocked to the ground. The noise I have heard is Sonya's dog, Trooper, jumping through one of the screens on the porch. In hyperspeed he jumps on my chest and knocks me to the ground. As I lie on my back, trying to piece together what has happened, Trooper takes bites out of my stomach and left thigh, making his way to my "secrets." Suddenly, Trooper stops, jumps off of me, and runs back inside the house through the screen he jumped out of in the bottom of the door.

I lie in the dirt still trying to come up with what has happened. Sonya has sat there motionless the whole time. Her reaction time is just as bad as mine. She begins to cry as she looks down to see I am bleeding from my stomach and thigh. I look down, and the sight of blood rockets me to the present. The pain strikes me a fraction of a second before I figure out I have been bitten. I jump up and run out of her yard, around the front of her house, and into the front door of my house. Mom is in the kitchen making dinner, and my screams interrupt the dinner preparation.

I am rushed to Sinai Hospital (about two hundred yards away, at the end our street), where I get a tetanus shot, and the nurses clean my wounds. The bites are not deep enough for stitches, but it feels like he sank his teeth into my soul. After a few hours, I am released with a souvenir syringe, absent the needle, to use as a squirt gun.

For the next few weeks, Mom makes me drop my pants to show all her friends my wounds. I repeatedly stand with my pants around my ankles and my Fruit of the Looms covering my last ounce of dignity as each puncture mark gets pointed out. No more are my "secrets" a secret.

I never see Trooper again after our one-sided wrestling match. My afternoons seem empty without him. I miss kicking at his face through the fence, or throwing a tennis ball or dirt at him from the safety of my side of the fence. My friends say the reason Trooper bit me was because Sonya's family used to feed him gunpowder to make him mean. I always think it was because Trooper was just paying me back.

Life on Whitcomb Street creates my first memories of relationships outside of my family. The days are spent creating memories like the Trooper story, being a kid, and enjoying the fact that I am surrounded by kids like me.

Other kids come and go in the neighborhood over the five years we live there. The Holmes family, the only all-white family in the neighborhood, lives on the edge of an old folk's home. Mr. Holmes is the director of the home. Their house shares a large yard with the nursing home. The yard is several football fields wide and long. They also share the outdoor pool owned by the nursing home. We only swim in it a few times because we are afraid swimming in the pool will make us smell like old people. The Holmes children are not an accepted part of our group, so I don't see them much. When they do come around, they play with us but are not a part of us. At the time I rationalize that this is because they don't live on the block. Looking back I am more convinced they were excluded because they were white.

Fat William is a temporary character who shows up on our street. He comes around primarily to play basketball. We have the only rim on the street, so our backyard is very popular. Many times we return home from a trip to the store to find our backyard filled with tall teenagers—most of whom we don't even know. Fat William is very generous with our court. I don't know Fat William's last name, and "William" is never said without "Fat" preceding it. Fat William annoys me. He is a "user." I don't connect with him because he is only after my stuff and not a relationship. I am relieved his status is only temporary.

One hot summer day, we pull up in our driveway after church and see Fat William high up in our backyard cherry tree. He is about twenty feet up and eating cherries right off the branches. Mom immediately yells for him to climb down. I am amazed at how agile Fat William is as I watch him disembark from the tree. He must have the mind of an engineer to know exactly which branches will support his three-hundred-pound frame. As his last chubby foot touches the ground, Mom passionately tells him not to return unless someone is home. Her passion can be heard four houses away. William exits the backyard unaffected by Mom's yelling. I stand by Mom with my ears still pinned back from her verbal assault. His bravado seems pretty impressive to withstand Mom's lashing, but Fat William never comes back; apparently he is more affected than I first think.

My best friend, Tony, lives with his mother and father. He is brought up to be very respectful of adults, and I like that about him. He would never get himself in the position that Fat William did. Tony knows if word got back to his mom that he was being disrespectful, life at the Herb household would be tough for him. He has his limits. Tony never participates in the potentially life-ending games, like "five fingered discount," that Fred and Marcus do. Tony knows if he did, this could mean the end of his life if his parents found out. Tony is a balance of tough but respectful, confident but not mean.

These colorful characters and scenes paint my everyday life. In them, I chisel out the beginnings of my identity. They help define for me what it means to be proud about being black. The pride that I absorb from them will protect me later in life.

At the same time, the risks and cost to the rest of the family are monumental.

Life for my brothers James and Matthew on Whitcomb is tough. They are the only two white boys on the block. Lisa doesn't come out much to play. The street is dominated by boys, and there are no girls her age, so she stays inside most of the time. Occasionally, she catches me inside, taking a break from the outside, and she experiments with my hair. I become her life-sized doll. She attempts to braid my long hair a few times and even figures a way to put rollers on my head. After a night of sleeping on the metal hair rollers, exchanging pain for sleep, I opt out of Lisa's beauty school. She retires as my hairdresser and assumes the role of my protector. If anyone messes with me, I know my big sister will take care of him or her. Tony assumes this role as well when Lisa isn't around.

James and Matthew are picked on for being the minority. James is more of a fighter, so after a while they leave him alone and take the path of least resistance. Matthew is often chased and terrorized. He routinely runs into the house in tears because one of the kids has threatened to kick his ass. I am the smallest of the kids we play with, but I never get those kinds of threats. I am part of the majority, so the oppression that Matthew and James are subjected to doesn't seem as real to me.

The whole family becomes a target. It seems like a weekly occurrence to have an uninvited guest/thief in our home. The most disturbing burglary comes one Friday night.

Friday nights are family night, and we usually make popcorn and watch our favorite show, *The Brady Bunch*. This Friday is no different. We have finished watching *The Brady Bunch*, and we are being tucked into bed by Mom and Dad.

The episode we just finished watching was the one where the Bradys go on vacation to Hawaii, and Peter finds an idol that he hangs around his neck. Peter is told by the island natives that the idol is cursed. While lying in bed with the idol around his neck he says sarcastically, "Bad luck, come and get me." Less than a second later, a large hanging falls off the wall and barely misses Peter.

That night I imitate Peter and say the same words when I go to bed: "Bad luck, come and get me." Bad luck shows up a few hours later.

In the early-morning hours, Mom hears a noise that wakes her up. She immediately wakes Dad. Dad, caught halfway between consciousness and a dream, rationalizes that the noise was probably Lisa going to the bathroom. Lisa's room is down the hall from their room. We boys share the large basement, which is sectioned off with paneling.

Although Dad is satisfied with his answer, Mom is not. Mom persuades Dad to go check it out. Dad checks on Lisa, but she is sound asleep—until he wakes her up. When he checks the front door, it is unlocked. Dad assumes that he forgot to lock the door the night before, relocks it, and heads back to bed. On the way back to bed, Dad notices a light on in the back room that we use as a family room. Dad again assumes it is an oversight and walks back to shut the light off. As he enters the room, his eyes find the empty space where the family TV used to sit.

Instant confirmation! There was someone in the house, and Dad isn't sure if they are still there or not. Dad calls the police and then hurries to check on us boys. We are fine and alone. It appears the noise Mom and Dad heard was the thief exiting out our front door. As they wait for the police, they survey the house and notice the screen in the dining room is on the floor. This is where the robber entered our home.

The police arrive, check out the house and the yard, and take the report. Later that morning, someone knocks on the door. A stranger stands on the front porch holding Mom's purse. He has found it while walking through Peterson Park, which sits at the end of our street. Mom's wallet is still in the purse, but the money is gone.

This is the purse that Mom always puts on the upholstered rocking chair by the side of their bed. She put it there the previous night, as always. Our guest came into my parents' room and took Mom's purse, which sat just inches from her head. If the intruder wanted to, he or she could have killed my parents that night.

Soon after this, on a Saturday night as we sleep in our basement bedroom, I wake up to lights bouncing off the ceiling and walls. I hear shouting that sounds like the voices are in the house. As my eyes focus, I can see lights in our backyard through the basement windows. The Detroit police are running through our backyard shining their flashlights in every corner. The neighbor saw someone in our yard and called the police, and now the police have arrived to attack our backyard. They are shouting to each other as they check the yard and behind the garage. But the visitor already exited prior to the police's arrival.

The unwanted visits continue. Over Christmas vacation one year, Mom and Dad arrange a Christmas away from the chaos on Whitcomb. We spend part of the holiday in a cabin in the woods surrounded by white cold. The cabin is bare, but it is an inexpensive way to spend a vacation, and rides down the hills on our toboggan make the bare cabin worth it. The hills seem like they start just outside heaven and end just above sea level.

We leave the dog at home and entrust the feeding to Tony. He comes in the house two to three times a day to feed the dog and let her out to go to the bathroom.

After several days of sledding, tobogganing, and enjoying family time, we leave the winter paradise to return to our dog and warm house. As we walk up the front walk, lying on the cement are several clothes hangers partially buried under the fresh snow. Each of us kids walks by the hangers and pauses to make sure what we see is correct. The thought of picking them up never bleeps across our radar. Mom bends down to pick up the hangers as Dad opens the front door to find the house is torn apart. There are clothes everywhere, furniture is turned over, and dresser drawers are all over the house. The TV is gone again! The house is in such a mess, it is hard to recognize what is missing and what is just out of place.

The police are called, and they come, inspect the house, dust for fingerprints, take a list of the missing items, and leave. We never hear from the police again, and all that has been taken is chalked up as a loss.

The nights on Whitcomb Street are always unpredictable. I am not afraid, but I know anything can happen and often does.

One night at about 11:00 p.m., our phone rings; it is Tony's father. He lets Dad know he just saw two figures creep into the space between our bushes and the large picture window in the front of the house. He explains to Dad that he has his shotgun pointed at the two shadows, and he is standing on his front porch after having loudly requested that the two shadows "freeze, or I will blow your heads off."

Dad steps out onto our porch, and there in the bushes, afraid to breathe deeply, are our friends Marcus and Frank.

They are scaling the house, hoping to reach the bathroom window to get a glimpse of Lisa coming out of the shower—and it's not the first time. Just a few weeks ago, Lisa came screaming out of the bathroom after seeing two sets of eyes peeping in the window.

Dad asks Mr. Herb to lower his shotgun. Marcus and Fred are sent home and told not to come back. Dad doesn't have the energy to call the police again.

It seems like the police know us by name, as many times as we have to call them. Reflecting back on this time, I never recall seeing a police car at anyone else's house but ours. I never remember anyone saying anything about being robbed. As I have become an adult, able to do some deductive reasoning, it's become easy to see who was robbing us. It had to have been our good friends. They knew our schedules, they knew when we went on vacation, and they knew exactly where in the house we kept the TV. They knew all this because we told them and invited them in several times.

These intruders, thieves, and terrorists were the people we called our friends. Fred, the friend we gave a middle name, Marcus, and some of their friends saw us as an easy target. They preyed on us and took advantage of us every chance they got. Dad would also tell me later he suspected Sonya's uncle participated in the free-for-all. I knew I didn't like "what's-his-name" for a reason.

I play these incidents back in my mind, wonder if Tony was involved in this activity, and always conclude he wasn't. It may be my emotions answering that question—I'm not sure. I still hold on to the hope that I knew him and that he and Marcus and Fred were cut from a different cloth. It saddens me to even suspect my close friend, but the opportunity was there, and the tempting call of the city was powerful.

During the time when we caught Fred and Marcus sneaking around the house, my feelings for my friends never changed. They were the kids I played with every day. They weren't bad kids—they had just done something stupid.

Life on Whitcomb, I know now, was chaotic. The constant risk that someone would and could break in and the harassment that my brothers endured made for a stressful life for my parents, I'm sure.

When the church became the object of a criminal's desire and someone broke in, it was less personal but more disturbing. It really showed what a desperate time it was then.

I remember walking through the church soon after the police left.

There is glass on the floor by the back door in the basement. The unwelcomed guest broke the long, thin window alongside the back door and reached in and unlocked the door. Once in, he went upstairs, we think. At the top of the steps to the right is Dad's office. The door to the office is locked, so he used the same method to gain entrance into the office. He broke the window on the side of the door and reached in and unlocked the door. This time, when he broke the window, he cut himself. It is easy to track where he went the rest of the time he was in the building because he left a trail of blood. It must have been a deep cut because the trail of blood is easy to follow, with large, circular dark-red drops.

He went through the small lobby of the office to Dad's desk in his office. He used a letter opener to pry open the locked top drawer of the desk. Nothing was in it but papers. He rifled through the side drawers only to find more paperwork and Dad's mouthwash. He exited the office and headed up the stairs to the sanctuary. He walked down the center aisle to the choir stand and the pulpit. Then he entered the small room off to the left of the altar where they usually prepared the communion. He found nothing in there and headed back down the center aisle and out of the sanctuary. From there he exited the church through the front double doors.

He exited the church with nothing of value. What he took from me was priceless.

After all the glass is swept up, the windows repaired, and the blood mopped up, I return to the sanctuary. During my peaceful walk in the sunlit sanctuary, I walk over to the choir stand. I look down, and in the wooden railing, I see a large red circle about the size of a dime. It is a drop of blood that has seeped into the porous wood. The wood is stained, and the blood drop will not come out. In my eight-year-old mind, this person who robbed churches is still here. He will always be here as long as the bloodstain is here. He took from me my peaceful sanctuary. I will never return there alone.

Many years later, I find out the peacefulness of the church was disturbed before the robbery. As the congregation became less white and more black, Dad felt as though many were questioning if he was qualified to lead a predominately black congregation. More and more, he felt he was being questioned as to how he could understand the issues of this black congregation. Dad had no concrete evidence of this, but it was something that concerned him. Because everything around him was so black and white, it caused Dad to think in a way he never had, and he struggled with this being reality versus paranoia.

Later in life I contract the same affliction.

Again, the family is caught between the races, desperately looking for a place to fit in. At home we struggle with just blending in. At Dad's place of employment, he feels the clock is ticking. As more whites leave and more blacks come, his fear of being less relevant becomes more real. In the neighborhood, we sit in the epicenter of the "kill or be killed" mentality. Our family is the slowest gazelle, and lions that surround us feast on us on a regular basis. To this point in my life, I am color blind because being a part of the majority shows me no disadvantages. My family experiences what I don't, and they are very color conscious.

Life on Whitcomb was hard. I see that now as I know a different way of life. In my adolescent years, I did not see the struggle because that was the only way of life I knew. To me everyday life included break-ins and Peeping Toms.

I sit here now and debate whether our situation was a "color thing" or a "life thing." In this neighborhood in Detroit, the law was, "You must strike first before life hits you." The break-ins were a combination of living out that rule and finding the easiest target to take advantage of. They saw us as easy. The question is, did they see us as easy first or white? The treatment that my brothers experienced was a "color thing." They were targeted because they were different and reminded of that almost daily. In the end, the balanced family life that Mom and Dad were searching for would not be found on Whitcomb Street. Whether it was a "color thing" or a "life thing" didn't matter. The desire to raise a family in a safer environment trumped the debate.

After five years on Whitcomb, it was time to move on, and God stepped in again to move the pieces on the playing board.

Our next move would show me a mirror image of the life I was living on Whitcomb.

The bishop who had saved us once before was in need of a new assistant. In the summer of 1975, Dad received a call to be the assistant to the bishop. It meant a huge promotion and a move away from Whitcomb and public school. We gladly packed, saying good-bye to the nighttime visitors and peeping Marcus and peeping Fred. We moved to an upper-middle-class neighborhood on the northwest side of Detroit. The new neighborhood sat only two miles away from Whitcomb, but the differences in the two neighborhoods made it seem like we had moved to a different planet.

With the new job and new house came a new experience for me. I would now be the minority in a neighborhood that had been happily white before I arrived. I broke the color barrier on our street and would learn a new way to navigate through life. The colorless world that I saw would become very colorful.

6

PROMOTED

The quiet two-thousand-square-foot house has a large yard with a basketball hoop, four bedrooms, a finished basement, and one and a half baths. The street is lined with large elm trees that create a natural canopy. The house is in foreclosure, and Mom and Dad buy it for $20,000. Everyone says that is a great deal, but it means nothing to me. All I know is that $20,000 gets me a better life.

I stretch out on my bed in the upstairs bedroom I share with my brothers James and Matthew. I still have roommates, but at least we are above ground. I sit at the window that looks out on the front yard, and I am amazed at the quiet. Sometimes I sit with the window open on a warm summer night and watch nothing, or I watch the moths fly up into the streetlight at the end of our driveway. Matthew has Ernie Harwell on the radio calling the Detroit Tiger game, and I breathe in calm.

We are only two miles away from the chaos we used to call home, and it feels like another time zone. The pace of life here is different, and the hour hands on the clock move slower. Life will be different here in ways I can't imagine.

It is September of 1975. I am eight years old, and the change is exciting. As we unload boxes from the moving van, a.k.a. the family car, a neighbor from across the street stops over. She introduces herself as Julie Tenbusch. She explains that she and her husband, John, also have a large family: three boys and one girl. Mrs. Tenbusch offers to pick us up from school the next day, so Dad and Mom can have more time arranging the new house.

It is a neighborly gesture to offer and just as neighborly to accept. It is even more neighborly to accept with the promise of sharing beer on the porch later in the week.

Mom and Mrs. Tenbusch will share a lot of Pabst Blue Ribbons on the Tenbuschs' porch over the next several years. There is community in this new neighborhood, and I like that a lot.

The next day, we are told to watch for Mrs. Tenbusch, instead of Mom, in the school parking lot. As agreed, our ride is waiting when the school bell rings.

I am nervous about meeting the neighbors for the first time. I lift a cautious foot into their dark greenish-brown Catalina. Mrs. Tenbusch is our driver, and her warm smile makes the first step into the car much easier.

I peer in to the backseat, and there sit four kids, three of which have the blondest hair I have ever seen outside of Cindy from *The Brady Bunch.* John has dark hair; he is the oldest, and he is the same age as Matthew, nine years old. Mike is the second oldest, and he is six years old. Mollie is the only girl and next in line. She is four years old, and the baby, Joey, is two years old.

John is the polite, talkative one and talks the whole two-mile trip home. I listen and say nothing. Lisa, James, and Matthew all join in on the conversation, and I just smile. At eight years old, I already know the inevitable conversation that will be had in the near future. The ride ends before the questions are asked, and we all spill out of the car with homework and books in one arm.

I carry in one hand my paper bag from lunch, which houses an apple Mom always sends with my lunch that I never eat. Later, I learn to throw the apple away after lunch instead of bringing it home just to be used again the next day.

I walk down the Tenbuschs' driveway, across the street, and up our new driveway. As I get closer to the large two-story house, it keeps getting bigger and bigger, and I keep feeling smaller and smaller. I walk through the front door into the foyer. At the old house, our foyer was our dining room.

The dining room is to the left after I walk through the foyer, and the living room to the right. Through the dining room, you enter the kitchen that has a built-in dishwasher and carpet. There is carpet in the kitchen, something only rich people have, I say to myself. Off the kitchen is a small dining area we call the breakfast nook. I have never heard of a nook or foyer prior to the new house.

Everything is new and big and exciting and scary and overwhelming and great. Soon after we arrive home, there is a knock at the front door. It is Mike and John Tenbusch, and they have brought the whole neighborhood. There is a legion of boys around my age.

They all yell into the house, "Hey, you guys wanna play Ditch It?"

"What is that?" Matthew responds.

John explains: Ditch It is a game where one team is "it," and they have to find and catch the other team. In Ditch It, hopping fences, running through neighbors' yards, and going over a block in each direction are all within the rules.

My initial excitement begins to fade. No way is Mom going to let us go that far away from the house.

"Can we go play?" I cautiously ask.

"Yes, go ahead," Mom surprisingly says with a smile.

The peace that I feel is not only felt by me in this new neighborhood. Already Mom is agreeing to things she never would've in the old neighborhood. Before Mom can change her mind, Matthew and I run out the door.

We are introduced to all of the kids, and it is time to choose teams. The standard is universal no matter what neighborhood you come from. We all stand in a circle, and each kid puts one foot in the middle. Usually, the oldest kid is the one who kneels down and begins the rhyme, touching each toe in the center of the circle.

"Ink, a bink, a bottle of ink, the cork fell out, and you stink." When he lands on your foot, you exit the circle. If we have ten kids, the first five counted out are on one team.

The teams are divided, and now we are ready to play. But Mark has to run home and change into his "fast" shoes.

As we wait, the inevitable questions slowly come out.

"So he is your brother?" The question is asked to Matthew. For a brief moment, it is assumed I cannot hear or see them looking at me.

"Yep," Matthew says without a pause.

The inhibitions present when adults are around are quickly shed in a group of young boys.

"How is he your brother?" they probe.

Again Matthew keeps the pace and immediately responds, "He's adopted."

"How come? What happened to his *real* mom?" This is the next question from another curious boy.

"His mom could not take care of him, so we adopted him," Matthew says, leaving no room for questions. His answer tells them, this is how it is—period!

Matthew and I have been through this conversation before. We know our roles. He is the big brother. He answers the questions, so I don't have to. I stay nearby and just look down until it is over.

As I remember this line of questioning, I see so many things wrong with it, but that is how it always went, almost word for word. Being described as "adopted" has left an impression on me. Never being able to be separated from the legal proceeding that said I was a part of the Hofmann family makes it hard to feel a part of the family. I grow up feeling like the son of Mom and Dad and brother of Lisa, James, and Matthew, but being described as adopted makes it feel like my name is followed by an asterisk. Part of my identity became attached to the adoption because it was stated in the present tense: "Kevin *is* adopted" instead of "Kevin *was* adopted." This was a tiny example of how adoption made me feel different when all I wanted to do was fit in. I didn't want special treatment. I just didn't want to be treated differently.

The questions about my *real* mother sounded funny to me. In my head the only mother I knew was the one who adopted me. My birth mother was the one who gave me up for adoption. Again, in this small conversation that happened over and over again, there were three parts of it that made me feel different and artificial. The first part was having the conservation in the first place. I know it is necessary, but in my adolescent years, it felt like they were asking, "Why does he have three eyes?" Immediately, I felt like I was a newly discovered creature. The second part was the, "He is adopted" part, and the third part was the "real mother" investigation. I have grown to hate that feeling of being different or singled out.

The last exception I have to this conversation is the explanation as to why I was adopted. The standard answer that was always given was that my birth mother couldn't take care of me. It is an answer to a question that provides no information. Many years later I would learn the real answer was that we didn't know. This vague response frustrated me because it provided no concrete answer as to why my birth mother gave me up. The true answer to this question was something I would search for over the next several years.

I have never known what not being adopted feels like. The lack of continuity in skin color in our family never makes my adoption a secret. But there is no shame in being adopted.

Back to the game. The initial conversation with a group of all white kids is uncomfortable because I am the only black kid. For the first time since I can remember, I am a minority outside of the house too. The safety of the majority is gone.

They conclude the question-and-answer session when Mark returns in his Chuck Taylor high-tops. I raise my head, the eyes turn away from me, and we start the game. We don't quit until Mom's call for dinner rings through the neighborhood.

Being the Jackie Robinson of the neighborhood, I am the first black boy that most of the boys ever socialize with on a regular basis; it is a learning process for us all.

Peter Gallow, one of the older boys, refers to black people as "colored," and he always follows it by pausing, looking at me, and saying, "No offense." I immediately learn that you can say anything offensive as long as you follow it with, "No offense."

Referring to black people as "colored" is not what offends me. It is the pausing awkwardly and singling me out that offend me. It is a constant reminder that I am different; I am not one of the group. This is the biggest change from the old neighborhood. Now I have to accept that I am the different one and am reminded of this often.

I quickly learn who in the group may say something that will single me out. When those friends are present, I am tense. I contract my stomach muscles in anticipation of the verbal body blow. It's never certain whether, in the middle of a conversation, they may say something that draws all eyes to me. Peter is one of those people. I am confused about friends like Peter. I do consider them my friends. I look up to Peter because he is very charismatic and likeable. I want to be his friend, and I want him to like me, but some of his characteristics I hate. Unconsciously, when he is around, I prepare myself for the "colored" reference. When it comes, I just want it to go by as quick as possible.

The conversation usually follows a similar script.

"Then this colored guy...oh, no offense," Peter says.

I respond by laughing or saying something like, "Oh, that's OK."

Peter continues, and the attention is quickly directed back to the conversation.

Reliving those conversations upsets me. They upset me because I gave Peter and people like him permission to refer to me in a degrading way. The color of the person's skin never had anything to do with the story. But the way Peter viewed this person as different was very similar to how Grandma used "they" and "them." It was a casual way of putting a person on a lower level. I understand now and partially understood then that Peter and those like him didn't do it to be mean, most of the time. I also understand that it was a learned behavior from those older than Peter, who taught him their believed hierarchy of the world.

As a child, I am often curious as to what the conversations are like in their homes when I am out of earshot. There are also some, and I think Peter is a part of this group at times, who will say things on purpose that they know are offensive just to see how I will respond. I can feel them shoot me a look after they have said something, just to gauge my reaction. I purposely look away and try to act unaffected. I don't want to give them what they are looking for. It is often this exhausting mental game of chess. I respond to the move they make, and they make another move, and I respond again.

The Tenbuschs, the family who picked us up from school, are great at making me feel welcome, and I never get that kind of awkward feeling when I am with them. The only time it is ever mentioned is soon after we move in.

Mike and I are walking down their basement steps, and Mollie looks up at me from the basement, turns to her mom, and asks, "How come his skin is so brown?"

Mrs. Tenbusch shoots back, "Mary Elizabeth!" (Mollie's full name).

That is the end of it. Mollie is a curious four-year-old, so this doesn't bother me, and Mrs. Tenbusch's embarrassment and concern for my feelings let me know this is a safe place to play. Not having to flex my stomach muscles in anticipation of something wrong being said is a luxury.

I spend a lot of time over at the Tenbuschs', and soon I am treated like one of their kids. If I do something wrong, Mrs. Tenbusch lets me know. She yells at me like one of her own children, and getting in trouble has never been so comforting.

Unfortunately, not everyone is so considerate of my feelings. To the right of the Tenbuschs live the Galanos. They are first-generation Americans from Argentina. Jose, who is a year younger than me, is their only child. Jose does not like me. I am not sure why at first, but soon it becomes very clear.

We play football on the front yards across several houses. One day, while playing football, my team is celebrating a touchdown. Jose, who is on the opposing team, walks toward me and quietly says, "Up your nose with some panty hose...some black ones." The way he says it and the way he looks let me know the comment is more about race than panty hose. Even at eight years old, I find that racism is very recognizable.

This type of racism surprises me. When I look at Jose on this cool fall day, I notice he has kept his summer tan much longer than the other white kids. In fact, he maintains a tan throughout the whole year, just like me. We are each a child of color, but he is able to pass for white.

My response to his comment is quick. The training from my prior neighborhood shoots through me like electricity, and instinctively I raise my middle finger. The violent presence of my middle finger causes Jose to dart into his house and tell his father. I am standing on the football field as Mr. Galano calls Peter over. The older man's eyes never leave me as he instructs Peter to straighten me out and goes back inside. The fact that he won't even speak directly to me says a lot. In his mind I am not worthy of his speech—and I am convinced he is right.

Peter politely explains that I have to be careful about what I do and say to Jose. Jose has the habit of running in and telling his parents about everything. This usually is followed by an irate

Mr. Galano appearing at their front door. They scold the mean child that has hurt Jose's feelings and disappear back in to the house.

This mixed message causes me to question Jose's motivation. Is he just a spoiled only child, or is it because I am black? This begins a change in thinking for me. In the old neighborhood, if someone didn't like me, since they were black, I never questioned if their dislike for me had to do with my skin color. In the new neighborhood, this questioning of motivations appears and takes up residence in my head.

Incidents like this with Jose happen over and over and over. I am not the only one who is targeted, so I flop back and forth between possible reasons for this extra attention.

Over the next few years, through our own socialization, we kids learn to work things out. We all learn to live with each other and negotiate how to interact. Gradually, I move away from being the "colored kid" to being "Kevin."

As kids, we still fight over who is out at home plate, who fouls whom, who cheats at what game, and who is the best player on the Detroit Tigers, Sweet Lou Whittaker or Alan Trammell. But these fights last only as long as it takes us to come up with another debate.

Many times back then as we kids learned through our interactions, I would look up and see Mom's glasses in the dining-room window. For years I thought she was only watching us play. Now I know she was watching to see how I was doing in this new environment. She and Dad made another extreme choice in moving us to this new neighborhood, and she was making sure I was doing all right. Youth has a way of working things out.

Because we were young and our prejudices were not deeply rooted yet, we found out they were reversible. I also learned the prejudices that had been fertilized and watered for many years were almost impossible to reverse. Mr. Galano held on to his conditioning, and he had a hard time accepting me into the community.

One evening the summer of my tenth birthday, Mr. Galano comes over to speak to Dad. I answer the door, and Mr. Galano tells me to get my dad.

The thought of Mr. Galano at our door makes my stomach feel funny; something is wrong. I go to get my dad and then vanish into my room and pick up the closest toy to distract myself. The escape that I get through my imagination is shattered when I hear Dad yelling.

"If you don't get off my porch, I am going to put my fist through your face." The bass in Dad's voice scares me.

Mr. Galano decides to keep his face whole and walks back home.

Later, James tells me they were fighting over me. Mr. Galano came over to tell Dad that someone had keyed his car, and since I was the newest and darkest kid on the block, it had to have been me. Dad took exception to that.

That next winter, early on a Saturday morning, Mr. Galano has a stroke that leaves him paralyzed and unable to speak. Our parents are heartbroken and rush to assist Mrs. Galano in any way. Mrs. Tenbusch is a nurse, so her medical expertise and care are comforting to Mrs. Galano. Mom sends over dinners to be reheated when they need them. Jose is swallowed up by the commotion, and I don't see him again until summer.

I lie awake many nights, wondering if it was my prayers to God asking him to take care of Mr. Galano that caused this to happen. The relief that Mr. Galano will not be behind his front door waiting for me to make a mistake brings me peace. The relief that I feel causes me to feel guilty because I have gained my relief at the expense of another family losing their father and husband as they once knew him. Relief and guilt wrestle in my chest night after night. Eventually, I train myself not to think about what has taken place and the cost of it.

The summer of my eleventh birthday, Jose returns to playing outside with us. Surprisingly, he asks his mom if Mike and I can come over and play. Mrs. Galano allows me to come into her home for the first time. She is friendly and kind. She offers us cookies, but I am not comfortable enough to accept, so I politely decline.

After that initial visit, I come over more and more. Mrs. Galano softens toward me. I am not sure if it is because of what happened to Mr. Galano or because he is unable to object to me. I also ponder that it might be because I am not the monster she has expected. When I play with her son, she sees a black child as just a child.

The three of us, Mike, Jose, and I, often play with Jose's Star Wars toys in the front room. Jose has the best, most recent, and most expensive collection of all things Star Wars. Initially, a large part of the attraction to going over to Jose's house is his collection of toys. The more time we spend together, the more I'm able to see past the toys to a kid who is likeable. As I grow to like Jose more and more, the tragedy of what has happened to his father becomes more real and adds to my guilt.

Spending time with Jose in his front room watching *The Three Stooges* and playing together fosters an unexpected friendship. This friendship blossoms while Mrs. Galano takes care of Mr. Galano in the next room. As Luke and Darth Vader fight in the front room, I can hear Mrs. Galano talking to Mr. Galano. He lies in a hospital bed behind a partition just past the dining room in their breakfast nook.

Jose asks me a few times to come see his dad, but I am terrified of all the machines and noises that come from behind that partition. I also know Mr. Galano does not realize I am in his house, and it's better that way.

In the first three years of life on Shaftsbury, I learn lessons that last me a lifetime. I learn the training from Whitcomb Street has saved me. At eight years old, I am proud of being black. I am secure enough to withstand the new experience of being treated differently because I am darker than everyone else. This pride and security were instilled in me back on Whitcomb Street. What I learned about who I was and what it meant to be black came from those crazy friends on Whitcomb who looked like me. The training I got from Tony, Marcus, and Fred insulated me from this cold environment. The hits I take initially from my new friends simply bounce off me. The ability to detach myself from the situation saves me. The blows that could have been fatal are instead only flesh wounds. I am able to return the next day revived. Because I return day after day, I am able to build lifelong friendships with people who didn't like me much when I first moved in.

I still see Mom's glasses as she looked out of the dining-room window. If I could talk to the frightened mom now, I would let her know I'm gonna be OK. I am OK because you made the extraordinary choice to move to Whitcomb Street *first*. If I had moved to the white neighborhood first without the training from Whitcomb, I am certain I would not have fared as well.

I look back on how I continued to grow and negotiate my place in this new community. Although some situations were foreign to me and I often had to blindly feel my way through, foreign wasn't always a bad thing. It was the pleasant surprises that came from these new experiences that made the expected struggles easier to digest.

7

UNCONDITIONAL ACCEPTANCE

Shaftsbury Street becomes the backbone of my childhood memories. I experience a rich, amazing childhood that I would never exchange for Capone's lost treasure. The summers are especially filled with lifelong memories.

When I am ten years old, I inherit my older brother James's paper route, and every morning I wake up at about 5:30 a.m. to go to work. I dress with half an eye opened and roll down the steps and out the back door to the garage. The garage houses my red Town and Country wagon with the tall wooden sides. For a while, Mike Tenbusch, who has become my closest and best friend, accompanies me on my route. Usually, I take Outer Drive, which is one street over, and Mike takes Shaftsbury Street.

I wake him up by going to the bushes below his second-story bedroom window, where a string hangs down. Each morning I grab the string and pull. The other end is tied to Mike's wrist. As Mike climbs into bed the night before he slips the string on.

It is too early for me to ring the doorbell and wake the family, so this is the ingenious solution we devise. Later we ditch this idea when Mike becomes concerned that the string will get wrapped around his neck when he sleeps, and then in the morning, when I come to pull it, I will strangle him to death. Therefore, we create a new scheme that doesn't involve the possibility of death.

The new plan is much less complicated. I call his house and let the phone ring twice, and then I hang up. If Mike hears it, he gets up and joins me outside. Some days I do the route alone because Mike doesn't hear the phone ring. I suspect Mike hears it some days but opts for more sleep. He helps me for free, so I can't complain. Most days, Mike is walking out his front door at about the same time I am exiting my house.

On these early mornings, we meet up after we each do our assigned section and walk back home. During the week, we return to our own homes and go back to bed. We are usually asleep again by 7:00 a.m. At about 9:00 a.m., we wake up, and the day is ours. Our parents work during the day, so we are left to create whatever fun we want.

On Saturdays, we sleep in until 6:00 a.m., deliver the papers, and both return to my house, where Dad cooks pancakes, waffles, or French toast for breakfast. Saturdays and summers are great on Shaftsbury street.

The days are spent playing outside all day. Each day is a different experience. Some days, the kids in the neighborhood gather to play baseball. Home plate is Mike's front walk, and the outfield is our front yard. We play over hand, moderate pitch with a tennis ball. If you hit it onto our roof, directly across the street, it is an automatic home run. My older brother Matthew and Mike's older brother John hit several, Mike hits one, and I never come close to the roof. Baseball will not be my ticket out of the middle class.

Usually we are able to gather enough bodies to cover every position. If we run short, we play "pitcher's mound." This means that if you hit the ball and the pitcher is on the mound with the ball before you make it to first base, you are out. We have some games that would make the Detroit Tigers envious.

Some days we play whiffle ball or stick ball, or we race on our bikes. Once we get the ingenious idea to play Evel Knievel after watching him attempt a jump over some buses on *Wide World of Sports*. We build a ramp out of a sheet of plywood Dad has lying around in the garage and some bricks the Tenbuschs have behind their garage. Mike is Evel Knievel, and our friend Jose, Mike's sister Mollie, Mike's younger brother Joe, and I are the buses that Evel will jump. We lie down in front of the ramp, and Mike gets on his bike. He starts two houses away and comes rocketing down the sidewalk. He hits the ramp perfectly and clears us all.

At this age, we never entertain what failure would mean. John, Mike's older brother, calculates it much better than we do; with one punch, John urges Mike not to do it again. Mike takes John's advice.

Our summer days are filled with a lot of testosterone and very little common sense. One day we take the ladder from the Tenbuschs' garage up to their second-story balcony. We use the ladder to get on to their roof and walk around. One wrong step and we could have a fast trip to the yard two stories below. Again, failure is never considered.

More idle time leaves us to create our own entertainment. Mike and I decide to play assassins one day. I borrow my brother James's BB gun, and from my parents' second-story bedroom window, we take aim at Jose and his friend standing across the street in Jose's driveway. I lift up the screen enough to slide the barrel of the gun out. Mike takes aim and shoots once as Jose is walking in the side door. We quickly retract the gun, close the screen, and erase all evidence. Mike is sure he hits his target, but Jose and his friend never react, so I am sure he missed.

Later in the day, we move on to shooting at the next-door neighbor's garage window from my balcony and spend the rest of the day doing things we know we shouldn't.

When it is time for Mike to go home for dinner, Mrs. Galano meets Mike as he walks up the steps to his front porch. She begins screaming at Mike for shooting one of Jose's friends with our BB gun. Mike holds to the code and instinctively denies any part in that. After about thirty seconds of screaming, Mrs. Tenbusch looks out the front door and calls Mike in for dinner, away from Mrs. Galano. Mrs. Tenbusch knows there is a strong possibility that Mike did what he is accused of, but she simply has had enough of Mrs. Galano yelling at her son, so she rescues him. She never asks Mike if we did it or not.

Our hot summer days are filled with swimming in our friend Peter's backyard pool and playing countless games of Marco Polo. We often go out to Southfield, a suburb of Detroit, where Mike's grandfather lives. His large property in Southfield is great for playing any game our imaginations can create. Mike's cousins, the Walton kids, live nearby, and they join us in covering every foot of the several-acre property. Every trip to Southfield includes a trip by Mike's Aunt Ruth and Aunt Theresa's small ranch home. They are old, gray, and gentle.

The parade into their home is always the same. One by one the kids, John, Mike, Mollie, and Joe, go over and kiss each aunt on the cheek. After my second visit, I am the last in the line and not sure how to greet them. Aunt Theresa reaches her worn hand out and grabs my hand and says, "Well, what are you waiting for? Where is my kiss?" I bend down and kiss her on the cheek as she sits in her chair in the living room. Aunt Ruth then looks at me and says, "Well, where is mine?" I kiss her soft, wrinkled cheek as well. From this day on they are "Aunt Theresa" and "Aunt Ruth," and I love going to see them. Again, I am welcome as part of the family, and this helps me to walk taller.

Being seen and treated as different makes me feel different and walk different. I am very shy and quiet. Oftentimes I just want to go unnoticed because then attention won't be drawn to me. Being around strange people in an all-white environment makes me nervous. My stomach muscles stay tense, waiting for someone to say an off-color comment that will bring all eyes to me.

In this small ranch house in Southfield, I can exhale. It is another safety zone where I can just be a kid, and color doesn't have to be involved.

The importance of being around people like the Tenbuschs, Aunt Theresa, and Aunt Ruth is paramount. They feed into my self-esteem. Being surrounded by people who build me up becomes just as important as containing my interaction with those people who chip away at me.

My grandmother from my dad's side does a beautiful job of building me up. My dad's mom is a remarkable German woman who seems to be stolen from one of Mother Goose's fables. Grandma has a comforting thick German accent. She is one generation from Germany, and she settled in a German community in Cleveland. Visits with her are frequent and filled with baked goods, great German food, and no color.

When I sit next to Grandma on her couch, which she calls a Davenport, with the delicate doilies draped over the top of the couch, I feel connected to her. She treats me like my brothers and sister and makes me feel wonderfully normal.

Grandma knows what it is like to be treated differently. Her thick accent gives her away whenever she leaves her safe German community. She knows what it is like to be judged and discriminated against. Because of that experience, I think Grandma is sensitive to my experience. Legally, because of the adoption process, I am her grandson. Emotionally, I feel like her grandson, no different from my brothers and sister.

When I look back on it, that statement is probably not true. Grandma showed some favoritism toward me. She paid a little extra attention to me, and I always thought it was because I was the youngest. The most beautiful thing is that it never occurred to me she was showing me extra attention because I was black.

My thinking while with Grandma never involved color. She gave me more than what I desired, as did Mrs. T, Aunt Theresa, and Aunt Ruth. They saw the need in me to be treated like everyone else.

These safe zones created by these women and my family were imperative to my development. The normal childhood games and experiences combined with loving people began to dissolve my struggle to fit in.

As the summers ended, I would go back to a different way of life that I would now have to incorporate into my new life.

8

ALLIES

The summers end with school shopping, and I go back to my double life. I return to the private Lutheran grade school, which is pretty much all black, and then after school I return to our white neighborhood.

At school, I learn to talk black to fit in with my black friends. For the most part, it works. I am not as smooth as most in my class, but they accept me most of the time. Occasionally, one of my classmates will point out that I talk "proper." This is a polite way to say that I sound white. To this point, I have learned because I look black, I have to find a way to be accepted in the black community because there is no chance I will be included in the white community. Reality has shown me there is a huge gap between the black and white communities, and if I fail to be accepted in to the black community, I will get swallowed up by the gap between the two races. Choosing a side becomes necessary.

Grade school is an interesting racial balancing act. As the whites are quickly leaving Detroit for the suburbs, schools like my school are quickly changing from a predominately white student body to a predominately black student body. The teachers do not change. They are all white, and not all of them meet the change from teaching a predominately white student body to a predominately black student body with enthusiasm.

The school principal is Mr. Lawrence Schmidt. He is also the math teacher for the seventh and eighth grades and the meanest man I have ever met. Mr. Schmidt is an old-school Christian who believes in corporal punishment more than he believes in Jesus.

It appears he is trapped in the middle of the color shift, and no one has bothered to send him the memo. He is caught overseeing a school he would rather not. His lack of patience for his black student body is obvious.

He and his wife, who also teaches at our school, and their four kids are a large part of the school. Mrs. Schmidt is much more accepting of their situation and does a better job of being comfortable around the colorful student body. She is likeable, and I wonder how she tolerates Mr. Schmidt.

On many occasions, Mr. Schmidt loses his temper and strikes a student with his bare hand or with the yardstick he keeps at his desk for just this purpose. In extreme situations, he uses a one-inch-thick cutting board to strike students as well. The stories of Mr. Schmidt and his quick hand are legendary. I never witness it, but in a school of three hundred students, the stories travel quicker than the speed of light.

I do witness his explosive anger, which he carries with him like a sack lunch. He terrifies me and the rest of the student body.

I know enough not to make direct eye contact with Mr. Schmidt when walking down the hall. He often stands outside his classroom between classes, making sure there is no horseplay. I realize horseplay can endanger your life.

In my elementary mind, something about him is not right. He seems to be in a constant state of anger. The way he speaks to us if we forget a homework assignment or fail a test is borderline abusive. Your grade or performance is never private, and he shares his displeasure openly about how you perform in his class.

I dislike math, largely because of Mr. Schmidt. The fear of being ridiculed makes it so much harder to respond correctly when called upon in class.

One of Mr. Schmidt's requirements for math class is that we take and pass a multiplication-and-division test. If we fail it, we have to continue taking it until we pass. It seems I have taken this test thirty times, and each time, the stress of knowing that if I don't pass I may witness the rage of Mr. Schmidt's hand makes it even harder.

Now I must take it again. I study and study, and I just don't get it. I go in and I take the test and I flunk it *again!* Mr. Schmidt sends a note home that has to be signed by my parents and says something like, "Your son is an idiot and will never pass math." Realistically, the note probably says something like, "Your student has failed to pass the required math test. Please sign and return this note to verify you are aware of this." I am given the note and told to share it with my parents, and I have every intention of doing so.

In my haste to drop my books at the front door and race out and play, I forget about the note and also forget to have my parents sign it later that night. The trauma of the situation must block it out of my mind. Terror and panic attack me seconds before math class the next morning when I realize the note is unsigned. The realization that an unsigned note could get me knocked to the floor sends a rush of blood to my heart. My heart rate triples in a second, and I am sure everyone around me can hear my heart clanging against my rib cage. I call on God, Jesus, John the Baptist, and even Noah to help me out of this situation. I pray for a flood. I pray for the walls of the school to fall, and I pray for the seven plagues, but God ignores me.

When class starts, Mr. Schmidt asks those of us losers who have failed yet again to come up and give him our notes. Again, he doesn't phrase it that way, but that is how it is translated in my head. I freeze in my seat and pray that God will strike Mr. Schmidt with temporary blindness.

Nothing.

How about permanent blindness?

Still nothing.

God chooses not to grant my request, and Mr. Schmidt calls me to his desk. "Mr. Hofmann, I need your note."

Quietly and absent of any self-esteem, I reply, "I forgot it." I purposely stand on the opposite side of the desk, out of reach.

Mr. Schmidt slowly looks up from his desk, and I see the blood rise up his neck into his face and forehead. He looks like a thermometer, and I am convinced the mercury is going to explode out of the top of his head. He points to the door and tells me to go to the office and wait for him.

I do as I am told, terror racing through my body, and I play the scenarios in my head of how I will dodge his smack. I sit in the seat in front of the secretary's desk, waiting for him to appear. After what seems like six long years, he enters the secretary's office, walks by me, and into his own office. He calls me in and tells me he is sending me home.

Fireworks go off in my head. The "Hallelujah Chorus" plays after the fireworks finish, and I thank God for hearing my prayers.

I turn around and begin walking out of his office. He barks at me, "Get your mother on the phone, and tell her to come get you." I am prepared and happy to walk the two miles home but do as I am told.

I call Mom, and she is furious. To my surprise, I'm not the target of her fury. She is confused and upset and knows how difficult Mr. Schmidt can be. I assume parents are also scared of Mr. Schmidt, so I expect Mom to run out of her office at work to come get me. Instead, she demands that I put Mr. Schmidt on the phone. I give him the phone and go sit in the office chair in front of the secretary. Mr. Schmidt says very little in the conversation. He comes out of his office, his face red again, and he tells me to get back to class. It is over. Whatever voodoo Mom uses works. Mom has beaten the man I thought was unbeatable. The rest of the day, I stay a long arm's length away from Mr. Schmidt.

When I get home later that evening, I hear Mom tell Dad the story, and she is still hot about it. "How asinine can you be? Kevin is struggling in math, and your solution is to kick him out of school? Giving him *less* time in class? How does that help the problem?"

When she says it like that, it makes so much sense. Mom has a way of getting people to see things her way. She has made Mr. Schmidt, the math genius, see how this equation wasn't adding up.

The most frustrating thing about Mr. Schmidt's reign of terror is that no one seems to do anything about him and his rage, with the exception of mom's victory. We often complain to other teachers, and they don't say much. They give us the "I know, I know" look and change the subject.

Mrs. Scharfenberg, our seventh grade and English teacher, is our only hope. She is our oasis. Mrs. Scharfenberg is a thin, wiry woman who dazzles us with her entertaining stories and engaging style. She is a kooky but kind soul.

During test time, she sits behind her desk, and when the room is quiet as we are all trying to recall our grammatical rules, she cuts the silence with a loud declaration: "Someone is thinking about cheating." She stands up, grabs her big wooden pointer, and dramatically extends her arms and closes her eyes as if God himself is sending her a message. "Someone toward the back of the room is thinking about taking out some notes. Don't do it."

I never cheat in her class. I am too afraid God will tell on me.

She inspires us to be better than life tells us we can be. Even more importantly, she challenges Mr. Schmidt. She is our dragon slayer. Mrs. Scharfenberg is willing to do what no other teacher will do—stand up to Mr. Schmidt.

Mr. Schmidt and Mrs. Scharfenberg have a very tense relationship, and it shows. He is the most hated teacher, and she is the most beloved. I am sure he sees it as her siding with the enemy.

Oftentimes, students stay after school to speak with Mrs. Scharfenberg about what Mr. Schmidt has done to one of us. It becomes a regular routine. The student knocks on the door of the teachers' lounge. The door opens, and the smoke billows out from the freshly lit cigarettes. This is the seventies, when teachers' lounges are more like smoking dens. Mrs. Scharfenberg is summoned, and she appears from behind the smoke to listen and console the upset student. The student usually pours his heart out to her, telling her what evil Mr. Schmidt has done. She is our safe place to land, and at the end of the conversation she usually says something like, "This will be addressed."

She rises from the short counseling session, hugs the frantic child, opens the door to the lounge, and is swallowed up by the smoke. It is obvious she will have a discussion with Mr. Schmidt.

Mr. Schmidt is temporarily kinder and gentler immediately following this process.

It is here, among people like me, where I learn that sides are drawn. Under Mr. Schmidt's reign, we bond. He becomes a symbol of "The White Man" that the black parents warn their black children about. We gather together, and we talk about whites. They are different from us, and I am included in "us." It is here where the white in my blood dies off. I look black, even if on a lighter scale than most, and I am treated as black. My lighter skin does not win me any preference. As I choose the color of my uniform, I develop a sense of pride in my race. Being the underdog up against a weighted system, I am proud of the strong team that has drafted me.

We all teach each other to be leery of whites. Anything white is looked down upon. This lesson is learned in subtle ways. One such way is when I smuggle in a cassette that I taped of Steve Martin's *A Wild and Crazy Guy* album. In the back of the room, during lunch, I play the tape on my portable yellow Panasonic tape recorder. Several huddle around, and we listen to Steve Martin talk about sex and use bad language; both topics are forbidden, but being taboo to us makes them more attractive. We all let out muffled laughs and hope the teacher doesn't come over and see what's so funny. One of my classmates breaks up the party when he says, "Man, that white guy ain't funny. Now Richard Pryor, he is funny." Everyone agrees and loses interest in Steve Martin. No one chooses to listen to the unfunny white guy.

This white guy is still funny to me. I learn to listen to him at home and only mention that to my white friends.

Each night I go home to my white family. In my mind, they are not part of the oppressive whites whom we talk about at school. The Tenbuschs also get a free pass.

Race is not talked about at home. We don't openly speak about the obvious, and my white friends and I don't speak about race either. Mike, my best friend, and I ignore our different colors. Somewhere we learn talking about race with another race is uncomfortable and should be avoided. We tiptoe around the fat elephant that takes up 80 percent of the room.

Then one day, Mike returns my portable yellow Panasonic tape recorder. He borrowed it to practice a book report he had to give. He recorded himself practicing his oral report to see how long it was and to help himself memorize the report. The book was *Roll of Thunder, Hear My Cry* by Mildred Taylor. It was about the Logan family, a black family in the 1930s. The book depicts the prejudices that the Logan family endures because they are black in the rural South.

When Mike returns the recorder, his cassette tape is still in it, so I listen to his presentation. For the first time, I hear Mike talk about race as he describes the unfair the treatment of the Logan family. He is sympathetic and passionate about how wrong he thinks it is for the Logans to be treated like they are only because they are black.

This recording gives me the excuse and courage to openly talk about race with my best friend. I make a point to bring up race, and it seems Mike is relieved; the tension is broken. Our ideas and thoughts on race are similar. The lopsided society we live in, we agree, favors whites. We talk from the same side of the table, and Mike becomes an ally.

My life experiences continue to line up to help build a more confident me. I learn my racial identity and pride through osmosis. The kids who surround me in school feed me knowledge of the black experience, and I eat it up. I learn from them the differences between the races, and I learn of a culture I am not exposed to at home. In my crash course on culture, I find a more secure me. This environment at school builds on my prior training from Whitcomb Street, and I begin to settle in to who I am and how I fit in.

When I go home, I am now able to discuss what I feel and how I see things, and Mike lends a sympathetic and understanding ear. As Mike and I discuss race relations, our friend Jose often just sits and listens as we try and figure out how we fit into this system. The system that Jose was raised under is challenged, and he seems to be aligning more with our perceptions than the perceptions passed down to him at home. More and more, I see the environment around me changing, and my allies begin to outnumber my enemies.

Unfortunately, the enemies still exist.

9

UNDERCOVER

I sit at the end of the bench because that is where my talent has put me. Mom insists I go out for baseball because it will be good for me. I make it through most of the season, and I am still looking for the good. I sit on the bench with an African kid who is worse than me, and I find comfort in his inability. We are on the baseball team sponsored by the corner liquor store in a league organized by the local Catholic parish. We don't have cool names like the Tigers, or the Indians, or the Astros. We go by the businesses that sponsor us. My team is Parklane Cork and Bottle. The uniforms are white with green piping and a baseball hat that is green in the front and white mesh in the back.

We are nearing the end of the season, and I can't wait for this to be over. The coach is Mr. Shade, a mean white-haired grouch who's the father of our pitcher, Peter Shade. They are white, and so is most of the league. The African, whose name I can't pronounce; Gilbert, the Hispanic kid; and I are the only minorities on the team.

Practices are, at best, humiliating. The coach rockets fly balls off his bat to the less talented kids who play outfield. I chase more balls than I catch, and Coach gets to prove he still can hit a baseball. Each ball I miss is accompanied with some insult from Coach about how bad my skills are and how I should play the ball.

"Hofmann, you gotta get under the ball to catch the ball." His tone is harsh and degrading, and I am thinking, "If I get under the ball and miss the ball, I will get hit by the ball." I consciously choose insults over being beaned by the hard ball.

The games are an extreme extension of practice. Mr. Shade doesn't let up even though family is present. I play two to three innings each game because the rules say I have to play. If the creators of this league had not put that rule in the rulebook, I would have a permanent spot at the end of the bench. I play center field or right field or left field. This is usually the spot the African kid has been playing when they pull him out and put me in.

The outfield is good for me. I have rationalized that the ball can't possibly be hit fast enough that I can't see it coming. This way I can either fake to go after it or move out of the way; whichever way I play it, I will not get hit. As each batter comes to the plate, I go over in my mind what I should do with the ball once I get it. If someone is on first and there is a fly ball, I know to chase the ball after it gets past me and throw it to second. I have gleaned that through the coach's insults at practice.

Batting is a nightmare I hate to repeat. I am a small kid, and I fear that ball as if it is wrapped in death. At twelve years old, some of the pitchers in this league could throw this rock-hard ball through a barn door. At this age, unfortunately, the strength is there, but finding that barn door isn't always easy for some pitchers.

I bat near the end of the lineup. This means all the good kids have batted. The African kid bats before me, and the skinny white kid who stands two feet from home plate when he bats, bats after me. No matter what the combination, this group of three is not going to start a rally. There is really no incentive for me to hit the ball. If I don't hit the ball, I can go back to my comfortable seat on the bench—at the end.

The African kid is a magnet, and it never seems to fail. He gets up to the plate and stands motionless as the pitcher whizzes two strikes by him. I say to myself, "He is two-thirds of the way; one more and he can sit down in one piece." On the third pitch, I look away. I can't watch. I have seen it too many times before. I am praying the next sound I hear will be, "Strike three," but instead I hear a thud, followed by a gasp from the crowd, followed by a second of silence, followed by a faint whimper. The African kid has taken the ball on his left side between his seventh and eighth ribs. He limps down to first base, and as he passes by our bench, Coach yells to him, "Toughen up—shake it off!"

I force myself to take one step after the other toward home plate to go bat. My mind is fractured. When I get to home, I look down at first base, and the African kid's face is painted with his tears that are still flowing. I don't want to be him. I stand at the plate and concentrate on the ball. My eyes are glued to the ball, so I know where it is and how to get out of its way. The bat rests on my shoulder. There is no way I can swing the bat and concentrate on the ball. I stand immobile, waiting for three strikes or four balls. I will let fate decide what happens. No movement will be generated by me unless the ball is coming toward me. If it does come toward me, I may scale the backstop to get away. The pitcher sends three accurate balls my way, and I am called out and relieved.

Dad loves baseball. He is a big Cleveland Indians and Detroit Tigers fan. I am sure my skills disappoint him. He decides being an umpire in my league will be a good way to get involved in my baseball career. The daily insults and relentless pounding of my self-esteem are not enough. During the season, Dad umps several games, including a few of mine. I do find that Dad and I have a lot in common when it comes to baseball. As bad as I am as a player, Dad matches that with his umpire ability. I can now see how painful it must be for Dad to watch me play because when I watch Dad ump, I get a queasy feeling in the pit of my stomach right about where it joins my intestine.

When Dad umps the games I am playing in, I get the genuine privilege of sitting on the bench with Coach. The coach's son is pitching, and we are in the field. As the coach's son hurls the ball past the other team, straight down the center of the plate, and exactly halfway between the batter's knees and chest, Dad bellows out, "Ball!" After three or four batters get gifts like this, the coach erupts in to a symphony of words I am too young to say or hear: "Aw, you son of a bitch. That was a damn strike, damn blind ump." The coach is bright enough not to yell it. He says it so only I and the other bench dwellers can hear him.

The coach doesn't see the resemblance between the white ump and the black scrub next to him. I sit silently praying a foul ball will veer off and knock me unconscious.

I make it through the season, and unfortunately we make it into the playoffs and the championship game. This only prolongs this never-ending season.

The night before the game, Mike and I are outside playing, and Mike suggests that I practice my fielding. He hits some grounders to me and tries to get me excited about the game. We don't even attempt batting practice. I do a decent job of fielding, and the practice is called on account of darkness. I go to bed feeling prepared and hoping the sun will not rise.

The next day, I station myself at the end of the bench for the first three innings. Then I have to go to left field. The African kid comes out. I get no action in the field, and I am excited that no one is hitting to me. I run in from left field after the end of the fifth inning. One more inning. The score is tied, and I am just hoping someone ends this tie, so we don't have to go into extra innings. We are batting close to the top of the order.

For the championship game, Coach changes the batting order. The coach decides today to spread out the three sure outs. The African kid, the skinny white kid, and I are broken up in the batting order. I bat sooner than usual today.

Our catcher gets up and hits a single. Gilbert, the Hispanic kid, gets up and hits a single. The coach's son gets up and hits a single. The bases are loaded. The next batter gets up and pops out. It is now the batter before me and then me. My knees are beginning to tremble, and I am praying down heaven. I am pleading with God to let the batter before me hit into a double play. This season has been torturous enough. "Please, dear God, don't let me be the last out." The batter before me swings at three quick, blurred pitches, missing them all.

"Hofmann, you're up," Coach barks at me. The look of defeat mixed with anger consumes his face. I grab my helmet and bat and walk toward home plate. I get in position. This time, I know that if I accept three strikes without attempting to hit the ball, there is a good chance Coach will kill me before I make it back to the bench.

I grip the bat tightly, remembering to push my hands together. I have a bad habit of spacing out my hands when I hold the bat, and Coach doesn't like that at all. I dig my cheap red Beta Bullet gym shoes into the dirt because that's what baseball players do. I am still attempting to sell the idea that I am trying.

The pitcher winds up and zings a pitch at me. As it zooms toward me, I realize his pitches seem a lot faster from this view. I wildly swing. I hit air. "Strike one." The catcher throws back the ball, and I am determined not to swing at this next one. The pitcher flings it at me, and I stand motionless. "Ball one." Now I am thinking that if I can get three more balls, the potential winning run will be walked home. I can be the hero by just standing here. For once, no action in a sport could be a good thing. I ready myself to not swing. The ball comes at me and I freeze. "Ball two." I am halfway there. "Please, God, please." The next pitch comes, and I stick to the statue strategy. "Strike two."

"My God, my God, why hast thou forsaken me?" Now what do I do? I am panicking, searching for a way out, but the pitcher already has the ball, and he is winding up. This next pitch, what do I do? Should I swing or freeze? And I can't think fast enough, and I am trying to figure it out as the ball is moving closer and closer, and I don't have a solution yet. I concentrate on the ball, watching it spin toward me faster than the speed of light and in slow motion. I have to decide. "Lord, what do I do? Speak to me, Lord." The ball is crossing the plate, and I stick my bat out. It is a compromise between not swinging and swinging. The ball hits the bat and launches into right field over the head of the chubby kid whose talent has put him there.

I run like my pants are on fire, and the coach screams at me to run faster. I round first and head for second, and everyone is yelling for me to keep going. I tag second, and I stride for third. I land on third as the baseball lands in the infield. I stay on third, and the crowd, my bench, my friends, and my family go crazy. Three runs are scored, and I stand on third. Emotions fill my chest and try to escape through my tear ducts. My smile stretches from ear to ear, and I manage to dam up my tears.

I got it right.

The next batter hits me home, and I return to the bench a hero. The next batter grounds out, and our side retires. Peter Shade returns to the mound to end the game. He has pitched the whole game and is allowed to finish it. After one hit, we get three straight outs. We win the championship game.

We cheer, scream, and yell for the next five minutes because that is the only way we know how to celebrate. Coach Shade cuts our celebration short as he out-yells us all.

"Quiet down, quiet down—we still have to give out the game ball. That was a great game, a tough game, but we pulled it out, and we could not have done it without…the excellent pitching of my son, Peter." He hands his son the game ball and says nothing to me.

Sometimes adults are just mean and it has nothing to do with what color I am, but that isn't always clear.

10

MRS. MATZ & BRICKLEYS

It is third down and one yard to go. The yard we have to gain is Mr. Wright's front yard. He lives to the right of the Tenbuschs' house, and his driveway is the end zone. James, my oldest brother, hikes the ball and lofts a perfect spiral to Peter, who catches it at Mr. Wright's walkway and breezes in to the end zone. Peter raises the football above his head and then spikes it hard on the cement driveway. Just as the ball leaves Peter's hand, a look of fear consumes his face. As the ball hits the cement, it bounces to the right and lands on Ms. Matz's lawn. We all freeze. Ms. Matz's lawn is off limits. As soon as it comes to rest in her yard, a loud banging comes from her front window. The banging clearly shouts, "Stay off my lawn."

We know we only have twenty-three seconds to retrieve the ball, or she will storm out and take it. We all figure she has to have a room in her house full of our Frisbees, baseballs, tennis balls, and kick balls. Those types of balls are relatively inexpensive, so to lose them is not a big loss. The leather football is not in the same category.

We all look at each other and telepathically ask who is going to go get it. The time is running out, and we need to move, or the football will be lost forever. Wayne Scott, the crazy, loud kid with the unusual hazel eyes, moves first. He sprints wildly across Mr. Wright's yard and onto the forbidden turf. As he steps one foot on the grass, the loud banging on the window sounds again. Wayne jumps as his nervous body reacts to the sound. Now the race is really on. Ms. Matz is headed to the front door. As Wayne bends down to grab the football, she throws open her front door and yells, "Stay off my lawn!" Wayne jumps again and shifts into an all-out sprint. He grits his teeth, showing the shiny braces that cover his front teeth. Wayne lands safely on Mr. Wright's driveway with the football securely tucked under his right arm.

The cheers erupt, and we all pat him on the back or slap him five. Someone shouts, "OK, who's kicking off?" Our game resumes, and Ms. Matz returns to her seat at the front window.

Ms. Matz is a single woman, an elementary school teacher. It is easy to see why there is no Mr. Matz. She is about fifty-five to sixty years old and mean. She wears a scowl whenever we see her. After years and years of her being mean, her facial muscles have frozen in a bitter expression twenty-four hours a day. She lives with her elderly mother and drives a little red sport car. The fact that she teaches kids and drives such a cool car makes my head spin. These bits of personal information don't fit the monster mold.

To me, at age ten, Ms. Matz is as close to a monster as Bigfoot. We run from her like she has the power to kill with her cold stares. There is not a day that goes by in the summer that she is not pounding on her window or yelling at us. When that doesn't deter us, she calls the neighborhood security company to handle us.

The poor guy making minimum wage pulls up in his marked security car. He parks in her driveway and goes to speak with Ms. Matz. After a brief conversation where she appears to do all the talking, the plastic cop walks over to us, dressed in his dark-blue security shirt, jeans, and no-name gym shoes. He usually says something like, "OK, guys, give the old woman a break, and stay off her lawn." We promise to have better control of our toys, and he drives away. I am sure he knows it is nonsense, but it is his job to keep the community safe from toxic baseballs and Frisbees.

As we get older, she is less of a threat and more of a game. We purposely stroll across her lawn, and like clockwork she raps on the glass. The anticipation of the sound still sends us three feet in the air. The fear is replaced by laughing and dancing across her lawn.

Wayne Scott, who is her neighbor to her right, takes great joy in harassing her, and he organizes a committee to burn a cross or a swastika in her yard. No one is sure what either symbol means, but we know it will be a terrorizing and intimidating thing to do.

We decide to burn a cross in her front yard because the swastika is too hard to create. The cross is two lines. It takes less artistic ability. We will use gas to outline a six-to-eight-foot cross in the front yard, and then we'll light it. The fear of getting caught and punished negotiates it down to a one-foot cross in the back corner of her backyard made with lighter fluid. Wayne volunteers for the mission.

One quiet summer night, Wayne jumps the fence, clothed in all black. He quickly squirts the lighter fluid onto the lawn in the shape of a cross, lights it, and leaps back into his yard. We muffle our cheers so we don't draw attention to our terrorizing act. The little cross glows for about thirty seconds. The lighter fluid is eaten up by the flames, and the flames die quietly.

Burned into her yard is an outline of a cross, and it takes about three weeks for the grass to grow in and cover it. I always wonder what her reaction is when she comes across it while mowing her lawn. I'm not sure because she never mentions it.

Ms. Matz is one of my customers on my paper route, so I am forced to interact with her regularly. Each morning before the sun wakes up, I walk up her limestone walkway to drop off a paper. As I approach her front door, I begin speaking in tongues and praying that she is not up yet. I walk as lightly as I can, concentrating on making delicate, soft, weightless steps. Once I make it to the door, I softly and slowly turn the squeaky handle. I would sacrifice one of my siblings for some WD-40 at this moment. I pull open the screen door and place the paper down, absent any sound. Then I return the door to its prior position, and I creep away.

There are days when my luck cheats me, and she meets me at the door. She says nothing as I hand her the paper. No "Thank you," no "Good morning"—just the Look.

The way her lips turn up and her nose wrinkles gives off the appearance that a very foul-smelling object has entered her presence. My hormones have not started producing those odors yet, so it is not that I smell. Her disgusted look shows what she thinks of me without her saying anything. She looks at me and makes me feel small, inferior, subhuman, and repulsive. At this point in my life, my self-esteem is still maturing, and the wounds inflicted by Ms. Matz penetrate my armor and cause me to walk less upright and confident.

Occasionally, Dad hears how she treats us all, and he turns to me and says, "Is she just mean to you, or is she mean to everyone?" This is the same question I toss around in my own head over and over. My dad is asking me if I feel she is targeting me, and I don't know. I struggle with trying to define her for my own peace of mind. Is she a racist, or is she just a mean, bitter old lady? Could she be both? Could she be mean one day and a racist the next day? Is it the racism in her that makes her mean? It is comforting to know Dad is aware of racism and is trying to define her too. We still don't talk about racism in depth, but to know he sees it and struggles with it too helps comfort me.

As I begin to understand racism and its presence in my life, I begin to try and decipher each slight and snub I experience. This cerebral dialogue is a private conversation I often have with myself and one that I don't share with anyone. I am frustrated by the thought that the sight of my skin will stop some from ever trying to get to know who I am.

As an adolescent, I am trying to conceptualize and define racism without personalizing it. It is a daily struggle. I understand that Ms. Matz dislikes my skin more than she dislikes me. I understand that she dislikes the new black family who moved in around the corner and whom she doesn't even know, simply because they are black too. I try to explain to my heart that her bitterness toward me really has nothing to do with me. But it is often like trying to peel away a sticker from the paper backing. Sometimes you can peel it away with little to no effort, and sometimes the two are cemented together, and no matter what you try you can't get them apart. There are days when I can't separate racism from me, and the slights and snubs become very painful and personal.

I wrestle with racism but prefer to do it silently inside my head. When I'm confronted with it publically, it opens up a different set of challenges.

When I am about eight or nine years old, a group of friends and I go to the corner store, Brinkley's, to get some candy. I am the only child of color in the group. I am excited because it is my first visit to the store without any adults. I am given a quarter and told by my mom to hold my older brother's hand as we cross the busy street. Brickley's is a small corner store where you can purchase convenience items instead of going to the grocery store. They sell toiletries and candy. I am there only for the candy.

When we enter the store, I go right to the candy racks and quickly pick a bag of Gold Rush gum. This is gum that is packaged in the shape of little gold nuggets and comes in a small bag with a drawstring on the top. I have been envisioning this candy the whole time it has taken us to walk the two blocks to the store. I reach in my pocket, pull out my quarter, and give it to the old Italian woman who runs the store. I put the candy in my pocket and stand to the side of the counter, waiting for my friends to make their selections.

A few moments later, the Italian woman begins pointing at me and yelling. Her Italian accent is thick, which makes it difficult to understand what she is saying. The tone and volume of her voice make it obvious something is wrong, but I can't understand her. She then points at my pocket and holds out her hand. Then she points to the palm of her hand. I am still confused and shocked and scared. One of my older friends picks up on what she is trying to say. She wants me to pay for the candy in my pocket, the candy I paid for not five minutes ago.

It is plain to me I did because the quarter I was given is no longer in my pocket. I try to explain to the excited storeowner that I have already given her my one and only quarter. She demands I pay her for the gum, and in her broken English, she clearly says, "You steal!"

I try again to explain I have already paid for the candy, but she just keeps yelling, "You steal! You steal!

I stand there, accused of stealing, in front of my new white friends, and no one knows what to do. They are all consumed by picking out their candy, so no one was paying attention when I paid for my candy. I am still relatively new to the neighborhood, and they don't know me well enough to know if I would or wouldn't try to steal some candy. I stand on that cold concrete floor, frozen, not knowing what to do and envisioning the police coming and escorting me out in handcuffs in front of my new friends.

Thankfully, an older white gentleman in the store sees what is happening. He bends down and asks me, "Did you pay for that candy, son?" I nod my head because speech would cause the tears dammed up behind my eyes to flow. He reaches into his pocket, pulls out a quarter, and puts it on the counter.

My friends conclude their transactions, and we all return home. We never speak about the incident in Brickley's again, and I vow to never go back.

Looking back on that incident, I am convinced I was targeted because I was black. I still wrestle with wondering whether she did this consciously or subconsciously, but it doesn't matter. I truly think she believed either that I had already stolen from her or that it was only a matter of time before I would steal from her.

Instead of putting the blame on this bitter, shallow-minded Italian woman, I shouldered the blame. I thought there was something I should have done to prevent this incident from happening. I also was ashamed to bring that negative attention to my new friends. They were being linked to a thief, and I felt bad that they were given that association. That day in the small ten-by-twenty-foot store, I lost some height. Leaving the store, I walked out smaller than when I had gone in, and the concepts of race and racism continued to be cloudy with a chance of persecution.

A few years later on this same two-block walk, we would be confronted by three young black thieves, and I would have to question whether the stereotypes the Italian woman believed were reality.

11

TOUGH

Mike, his brothers, and his sister go to the neighborhood Catholic grade school. The Catholics are not immune to Detroit's racial shift; the color of their school is changing as well. Mike gravitates toward the black kids and develops the ability to talk just as black as I do. I still struggle with speaking proper, so we balance each other nicely. We are an odd pair, but people get used to seeing us together.

Mrs. Tenbusch always says, "Whenever you two are together, there is always trouble." She means it in a negative sense, but we take it as a compliment. Although we grow up in a quiet neighborhood, in the middle of Detroit, toughness is still important. We do not have much of it, so we cling to any reference to us being tough with both hands. The depth of our toughness is measured one Friday evening in the middle of summer.

It is a peaceful Friday night in August just before dusk. It is still too early for the mosquitoes and the streetlights but late enough for the sun to have disappeared behind our house. We get the OK to walk to the Dairy Queen. The DQ is on the corner of Six Mile and Outer Drive. It is two blocks up and one block over, and this walk, absent parents, signifies the freedom of summer. This is the first summer we are trusted to make the walk alone. I am twelve, and if I were as tough as I think I am, this privilege would have been granted much sooner.

Along with the freedom of going alone comes the absence of price restrictions. Before now, I always had to ask, "What's the limit?" The limit usually equated to a small cone. This summer, with my own money from my paper route, I can get anything I want on the menu. I already know that I am going to get a Peanut Buster Parfait. Mike will be getting the same. We have dared each other to step up to the window and proudly order "One Penis Buster Parfait." If said correctly, with a straight face, it can go unnoticed. If said incorrectly, with too much attention to the word "penis," it is certain the teenage girl behind the sliding screen will catch it. Either way the thrill of being able to say "penis" out loud and in mixed company really makes us laugh.

Mike and I are the leaders of our small group of harmless kids. Mike is ten and tall; Jose is eleven and round; Mike's sister, Mollie, is eight and quiet; and Joe is six and even quieter.

We slowly walk together, enjoying each other's company, as Jose, Mike, and I constantly shoot insults between us. Mike and I have a connection that doesn't include Jose, but we bring him along for the entertainment value. Jose is often the butt of our jokes. Sometimes he realizes it; most of the time he doesn't. But he enjoys being a part of the group and laughs at himself.

The three of us start a game of B. B. Butcher. The rules are simple: anytime someone says a word with a "B" in it, you get to punch him in the arm until he yells out, "B. B. Butcher!" The most skilled at the game can hit you so hard the pain takes your breath away to the point of not allowing you to get out "B. B. Butcher" at all. This translates into three or four extra hits. It is a thing of beauty to watch in the world of a twelve-year-old boy.

This is shortly before Jose's mom, Mrs. Galano, makes us stop because Jose is coming home with bruises up and down his arms. After the fun of punching Jay wears off, we talk about the girls we like in ways you can't when you are escorted by parents.

Mollie and Joe are two steps behind us and in a world apart from ours. We don't say much to them, partly because we are forced to include them on our trip. It is a condition Mrs. Tenbusch insists on if Mike is allowed to go. We agree but ignore Mollie and Joe the whole time.

We all near the alley that separates the quiet residential neighborhood from the businesses on Six Mile Road. The alley is a buffer between the transmission shop on the corner and the small corner house with the nice lawn. There are different laws on each side of the alley. The neighborhood side is calm and friendly. The commercial side is chaotic and cold.

We cross over without even noticing. We continue our stroll, and the new game of choice is talking about each other's mother.

"Man, Jose, your mom is so stupid, when the weatherman says it's chilly out, she runs outside with a spoon," Mike says. I convulse with laughter, and Jose joins me.

"Awww, Mike, that was a good one," Jose hollers back. Jose is always a good sport and appreciates creativity even if it involves his mother. Similar comments continue back and forth, and no mother is immune.

We arrive at the DQ and place our orders. Mike orders first: "Can I have a Penis Buster Par...fait?" He barely gets it out before we vibrate with laughter. Jose lets out a loud scream and laugh that come straight from his round belly. Tears roll from my cheeks as I try to order the same thing. The girl behind the screen is not amused. She shoots us each a disgusted look, which makes it even funnier. Through his laughter, Jose squeezes out his order, and we roar with laughter again. We wait for Mollie and Joe to get their small vanilla cones, and we stroll back home happy.

As we break from the large crowd that is lined up at the DQ, three boys about our age ride up to us on their bikes. Their leader comes right to me, inches from my face, and says, "Yo, man, give me all your money." I recognize one of them from the neighborhood, but the leader and the other one I don't recognize. They are three black boys a little bigger than me but not very imposing or intimidating.

Instinct tells me to be calm, confident, and tough to have any chance at keeping my money. It is one of those things you learn as part of your Detroit education. Deep inside, I chuckle because I know it is almost impossible to look tough eating out of a clear plastic parfait glass with a long red DQ spoon.

I give it a whirl. "Hellllll no," is my reply.

The leader is insistent on getting our money. He demands again in a harsher tone, "Give me all your damn money, man."

"Nah, man, it took me two weeks to get this money," I say, trying to sound unafraid.

We continue this exchange back and forth—all the while, we are still walking toward home. Instinct again speaks to me and tells me to keep moving.

Mike joins the negotiations by diplomatically telling them no. Mike reasons with them, stating, "Look, dog, this is my little sister, and you are scaring her. Why don't you just calm down and go away?" I look at Mollie, and I am convinced. Tears are filling her bottom eyelids and about to run over.

The three continue to follow us, demanding our money, and I continue to refuse to hand it over. Jose and Joe are quiet. Fear has spilled over from Mollie onto Joe. Jose is attentive, but his emotion is easily read: he is scared too.

We have now made it back to the end of our street. I need to get across the alley where we will be safe. It is one hundred yards away. If I just keep moving, I can get us all there.

Mike is close by my side, and I know if something happens, I can count on him to help me. I am worried about Jose, Mollie, and Joe. If these video-game junkies start to throw fists, these three are defenseless. We start to cut across the transmission-repair-shop parking lot at the end of our block. As we do, John, Mike's older brother, catches up with us. I have no idea where he comes from, but his timing is perfect. John is a year older than me but is bigger than our three new friends. The three speed away immediately, so fast it is like they vaporize. John doesn't even realize the three thieves were trying to cause us harm. John is shocked when we explain to him what has taken place. From a distance the negotiations between us and the robbers looked friendly. John assumes that, since they have left, we are safe to finish our walk home. John leaves us to go to Parklane Cork and Bottle to get some candy.

We are now fifty yards from safe ground. As soon as John leaves, the three boys descend upon us. We continue our walk. This time the mood has changed. They present themselves only partially showing their faces. They shield their faces by pulling the collars of their T-shirts up over their mouths. This small change makes them more intimidating, and they are more forceful with their demands. The friendly negotiations have been replaced with a hostile takeover.

They surround us and block us off with their bikes just a few feet from the alley. We are only steps away from the safe haven of our residential neighborhood, but we can't move without forcing a physical confrontation.

Mike and I only have prior experience fighting our older brothers. There are rules in fighting family members that I am sure these three won't adhere to. I can't see any way out. As I am trying to solve this problem, the leader reaches into his shirt and announces, "If you don't give me your money by the time I count to ten, I'm gonna start shooting."

I'm not convinced he has a gun, and his plea isn't forceful enough to sell me on it, but his acting convinces Mollie, who begins to cry. Joe remains silent and stoic. I want to hold onto the money, but more importantly, I want to hold onto my pride. Giving in to these three wannabe crooks hurts, but hearing the scared cries of Mollie hurts more.

I reluctantly reach into my pocket and give up the few dollars I have. Mike and Jose follow my lead and surrender their cash, as does Mollie. Joe doesn't move, and his size grants him immunity. The leader grabs the money from our hands and vanishes on his bike. His two flunkies stay long enough to apologize and shake our hands. It is a sign of respect, and this gesture makes me feel better. They recognize that we are not the punks they thought we were. There is honor among some thieves.

We cross the alley and enter the calm of the neighborhood. Mike, Jose, and I console Mollie and Joe. Their sobs disappear and are soon replaced with forced smiles as we try and make them laugh.

We all agree not to tell our parents what happened. Telling them what has happened will convince them that we should not walk to the DQ alone. We will become prisoners in our own neighborhood because of the actions of these three. When we get home, we sit outside on Mike's front porch and fantasize about what we would do if it happened again. We laugh and joke about how we would tear them apart. We joke about the "tough guys" who got our money and all agree they weren't very tough. We make fun of each other and how each of us reacted, and we enjoy the memories of the incident. This incident gives us "cool points." Since we survived the incident with only a few dollars lost, we are better for it. This incident will give us bragging rights in the future.

Jose gains respect for how he responded to the hold-up. He passes his first real test. He is now someone we can depend on versus the liability we thought he might be. He has grown up from the tattletale he once was. Slowly, the challenges of Detroit begin to creep into our small community.

The color of the three perpetrators doesn't translate into evil in my mind. I hear the murmurs of the adults around me who flee to the suburbs to get away from the violence of Detroit. Oftentimes this is translated into the whites leaving Detroit to get away from the blacks.

My mind doesn't equate black skin with evil. Fortunately, I see evil as actions and not skin color.

Shortly after the DQ incident, I accompany Mom to Grandland, a strip mall not too far from our house. It is located on Grand River near the Southfield freeway. It is a cold fall night. As we approach the grocery store to do the monthly shopping, a black man in his midtwenties walks toward us. He seems to be walking unusually close, which makes me notice him. He grabs the strap of my Mom's purse, which is over her shoulder. He calmly says with authority, "Gimme the purse, bitch," and he pushes off of Mom and sprints away with her purse.

We have a large family with three growing boys, so food is a major part of our budget. The grocery money is in the bottom of that purse in cash. As I watch the thief streak away, I think to myself, "Wow, that was quick. Oh well, we won't be getting that back."

Mom thinks differently. She sprints after him, screaming, "Stop him—he stole my purse! Somebody, stop him!" I am pleading with my muscles to coordinate their efforts to allow me to stay with my mom. She leaves me like I am running in cement shoes.

The purse snatcher dashes across Grand River, a busy five-lane road, to get away. All the attention of the parking lot is directed our way, including the attention of an off-duty police officer whose wife is shopping in the grocery store. He and some others take off after the man with Mom's purse as he disappears into the neighborhood across Grand River. Soon we hear two gunshots.

Then silence.

After a few minutes, two policemen walk back across Grand River, escorting the robber. The two shots we heard were warning shots that the police shot in the air. The audible warning stopped the robber cold, and he surrendered.

The police officer escorts the robber back to the grocery store. We are inside with the police officer's wife. They bring him close to the door, where I look out and see our robber. I notice he has a scar on his face. Mom is told she is not allowed to look at him because it may jeopardize the case. She will later need to go downtown and identify him in a lineup. No one is watching me, so I steal a peek out the store window and see the face of the robber. My eyes and brain memorize his face and the scar on his cheek. The scar makes him look meaner than I initially remember. I later share with Mom the information about the scar on his cheek, which helps her identify him in the lineup. I feel good about being able to help.

This is different from the DQ robbery. The potential violence with the DQ robbery was manageable. A few punches and bruises were all I would receive from that incident. The risk was minimal, and the threat matched the risk—all part of growing up as a boy.

The purse-snatching incident is more dark, threatening, and sinister. The assailant is bigger, and he sells the idea of being a bad guy better than the three DQ bandits. I do not let the purse-snatcher go so easy.

Over the next few weeks, eating is difficult. I know I have to eat, but my stomach is in no mood for food. Sleeping is also impossible. I see the guy on the inside of my eyelids when I close them. The violent way he invaded Mom's space flashes over and over. Fear takes up residence, and my toughness deserts me.

Thankfully, logic doesn't desert me, and I see these isolated incidents as incidents done by bad people, not black people. My racial maturity allows me to distinguish between the two.

This maturity and ability to see individuals for who they are began when I was three years old and moved to the black neighborhood. Because I had constant and consistent contact with black people, I grow up able to see the beautiful hues that come with black. I know good black people and bad black people, and because of this exposure, I understand good or bad don't genetically bind to one race or the other. I'm so thankful for this because if I had only been exposed to one stereotypical image of what black is, I wonder how that would have shaped what I see in the mirror every day.

12

ANOTHER BROTHER

We grow older, and the games of Ditch It stop. The baseball games are replaced with whiffle ball. Whiffle ball only requires three people—a batter, a pitcher, and an outfielder. Peter and a lot of the other kids leave Detroit and move to the suburbs, so finding enough players for regular baseball is tough.

Matthew, who is a baseball fanatic, invents a game where the distance you hit the ball in the air determines your base. We play on the yard to the right of the Tenbuschs' house. His fence, which separates the backyard from the front yard, is our backstop. If you hit it from there to the sidewalk, it is a single. If you hit it into the street, it is a double. The lawn across the street is a triple, and the sidewalk across the street is a home run. Hitting a whiffle ball that distance is next to impossible. If there is any kind of wind, the home-run ball is only a wish. Running through the neighborhood is now too strenuous and not cool. The yearly block parties we used to have are less frequent.

The block parties would take place on a Saturday afternoon. Our block would be closed off to traffic, and we would set up picnic tables in the street and play games and eat and socialize with our neighbors. They were some of the highlights of each summer.

Now the block parties are every other year, and the games are for the younger kids. The last block party we all ever attend is the year we have a visit from the Detroit police. A mounted police officer and his horse are commissioned to join our party. Mike, James, Matthew, Jose, and I sit around and watch as each kid is slowly paraded around on top of the horse. The officer in full uniform leads the horse up and down the street. We all joke about what we would do if we got on the horse, and how we would make it take off at full speed. It is a typical testosterone-filled conversation. Gradually the talk turns into a challenge, and Mike accepts. We dare him to ask to ride the horse and then make the horse run down the street away from the officer and the party.

Mike waits in line with the smaller kids. He towers over them, and they are half his age. Mike gets to the front of the line and climbs on the horse. The officer asks Mike if he has ever ridden before, and Mike confidently says yes. Mike is so convincing that the officer allows him to ride the horse without his assistance. The officer is tired of walking and is looking for a break, which Mike gladly provides.

Mike walks the horse slowly about ten yards. We are all on the ground laughing uncontrollably because Mike has conned this guy into trusting him. The ten yards turn into twenty, and then it happens. I am not sure if it is done on purpose or if maybe something spooks the horse, but the horse goes from a walk to a full gallop in less than a second.

The horse is now one hundred yards away and gaining speed. We all scream as Mike and the horse take a left at the end of the block and disappear. The horse is heading for Outer Drive, which is a four-lane roadway divided by a grass median. The speed limit on Outer Drive is forty miles per hour, and a collision with a car at this speed would most likely kill the horse and the equestrian.

Just before Mike disappears, he is bouncing up and down on the horse, and his long thin legs are flying up and down and kicking the horse with each bump, which just stirs the horse to go faster.

The police officer watches as his partner sprints around the corner and out of sight. He frantically jumps into his truck and pursues his horse and Mike. The horse gallops across Outer Drive, somehow avoiding contact with the cars that speed down the street, and continues on his journey, carrying Mike along as a hostage.

Our joke has now turned into panic for everyone, including Mike, who is atop this horse with no idea of how to make it stop.

As Mike passes stunned Detroiters walking down the street, he screams to them, "Hey, do you know how to make a horse stop?" He is never in earshot long enough to hear an answer. Then suddenly, just as suddenly as the horse began, he slows down and stops. The officer catches up with them, takes back his horse, and makes Mike walk home. The officer loads the horse into the trailer and never returns to our block party.

By this time, we have all sprinted around the corner to see the officer pulling away and Mike walking toward us with a crazy smile. We all cheer as he walks up to us. Once he's in the safe fold of our group, we all pat him on the back and give him a hero's welcome. It is an amazing way to end a block party.

Crazy stories like this continue to paint our memories, and color has nothing to do with them.

Childhood games are replaced by all-night basketball games in the Tenbuschs' backyard. As adolescence dissolves into our teenage years, we sit for hours and play horse, twenty-one, sign out, or two on two.

The games of Mike and me against our older brothers John and Matthew always end in fights, which end with Mike or me getting punched by our older brother. An older brother never takes losing to his younger brother well, and it is becoming more and more frequent.

When we aren't playing basketball, we sit on the picnic table in the Tenbusch backyard and just talk. We sit for hours and talk about nothing. Jose joins us as Matthew and John disappear into the business of their teenage lives. Jose slowly becomes part of us instead of the kid we keep on the outside.

We talk about the girls and women we are attracted to, and Jose joins in with us. Anita Baker, Sade, Irene Cara, Lisa Bonet, Vanessa Williams, and the ladies from the rap group Salt-N-Pepa all gets votes, and the debates as to who looks better are endless.

We talk about girls we know from school, and those we all find attractive are all black. The color barriers we all grew up under are now gone. The three of us sit there, hour after hour, never realizing how far we have come. Jose's dad still lies in the hospital bed in the house next door, and it breaks my heart that my friend has to see his dad like this for so many years. The boy I used to hate has become another brother to me.

13

DIVERSITY TRAINING

The spring of 1981 brings a joyous and sad occasion: I graduate from grade school. The school where I am accepted and where everyone knows my story is now over for me. I move on to the local Catholic high school to start my high school career. My grade school classmates all go to the local Lutheran high school or to the public college-prep high schools, Cass Tech or Renaissance High School. No one follows me.

I carry 110 pounds on my small frame, and I am shy and unsure of myself. The transition from the small grade school is not easy for me. I am used to a school with about 250 students, and now I go to a school about four times that size. The high school is small, as far as high schools go, but it is a big change for me.

The first day of high school is tough. I have never been the most fashion conscious, so I always seem to pick the wrong kind of clothes to wear. School-clothes shopping usually consists of letting Mom pick out the most clothes for the cheapest amount of money. This leaves no room for buying anything that is close to fashionable.

No one lets me in on the secret that most fourteen-year-olds aren't comfortable with themselves yet, so I feel like I stick out instead of fit in. The tag of talking proper sticks with me, making me even more self-conscious. I say little to anyone, and no one says anything to me. I miss the safe surroundings of grade school. I stand at my high school locker, dialing over and over again the combination, and I can't get it open. This only adds to the torture of my painful first day.

Walking home from school, I decide I won't be back again. Close to tears, I explain to Mom how my day was the worst day on earth—ever. Mom does not agree with my plan of not returning. It is not negotiable; I will go back the next day.

She assigns James to help me with my locker the next day, and that begins a string of better days. Good days and bad days find me, and slowly I make friends. By the end of the year, I am more comfortable. Having my brothers James and Matthew there helps but also means I have to explain our family over and over. Fortunately, by now, I am used to it, and it becomes a good icebreaker now that I am more comfortable being the one who was adopted. My story is unique, and over the last few years, this once-uncomfortable conversation has become one that gets me attention because so few have a story like mine.

Our high school was about 80 percent white when my sister Lisa started her freshman year five years ago. It is now the opposite, and the shades of the school are changing fast. Once again, James and Matthew are part of the minority, and I am part of the majority, but with a larger population, it is harder to hide my racial shortcomings.

My upbringing is different. I know little of the black traditions and culture compared to those who have lived it since birth, and in high school I get an education in what I don't know.

Initially, I hate to admit to my close friends my ignorance on things they know so intimately. Over time, these friends understand my upbringing and understand why I don't know certain things. I become more comfortable admitting I don't know people like Minnie Riperton, a celebrated female singer in the black community. I admit I have never seen movies like *Cooley High* or *Shaft,* have never tried chitterlings, and don't even know what they are or where they come from. Initially, my friends are shocked, but they remember I was raised by a pack of whites, and they understand.

They do not alienate me or shun me but take time explaining things to me. Two of my closest friends tutor me in black culture and instruct me in many ways, including dance.

Shortly before the homecoming dance my junior year, I divulge to Tyrone and Curt, my closest friends, that I can't dance. This is after I have asked someone to go to the dance, and we have all made plans to triple date in Curt's big Pontiac. Consideration is given to coming down with a cold or cancer, or to running away, but I decide this is something I have to tackle.

The evolving social side of me really wants to go, if only we could have a nondancing dance.

After my announcement, Tyrone responds, "You can't what?" He looks at me, and the look of shame on my face causes him to back off.

This is one stereotype I am so upset is not true. Rhythm is not attached to my genes. Instead, rhythm's evil twin, no body control whatsoever, is what my genes are constructed of. Tyrone is determined to prove to me I am wrong and that he can make the dancer in me come alive. Curt and Tyrone hold dance lessons in my basement. We turn on my small radio and pop in a cassette tape, and they attempt to teach me the Smurf and the German Smurf: the two dances every person of color can do, from Utah to Ethiopia. It consists of coordinated movements between both arms and legs, and my muscles go on strike. It appears the unions in my arms and the unions in my legs are in a dispute and refuse to work together. The end result is a huge work stoppage. Forcing it, even calling on scab workers to do the work in my arms and legs, fails. After hours of teaching, Tyrone declares that I have no rhythm and surrenders.

The hope that I had at the beginning of the lesson is shattered. I understand Tyrone's frustration, but his giving up on me stings a little. My pain is intensified when I share with Mike that I just couldn't get it, and Mike proceeds to make his body do what mine refuses to do. The white guy can dance, and I can't. What a cruel joke I am a part of. "My God, my God, why hast thou forsaken me again?"

Mom and I go out and purchase a new suit. The suit matches and is stylish. The tutoring is paying off. I spend seventy dollars on a pair of black leather Roots, the most "in" shoes, and I have a shot at pulling this thing off. Breaking a leg at this point would make my experience a success and help me avoid the dance snafu. Mom is appalled that the shoes cost more than the suit, but my paper route money is sacrificed for the shoes, so she is unable to object. The night of the dance, I am ready. Dancing will not be a part of my homecoming experience, and explaining this to my date is a painful conversation. She agrees to still go because all her friends will be there. I am relieved and slightly wounded. It doesn't appear I figure into her homecoming plans.

I have my date's corsage, and I am waiting for Curt's maroon Pontiac to pull up in the driveway. We have agreed that he will pick up his date, then Tyrone and Tyrone's date, and then me and my date. Our plan fails immediately.

Curt is an hour late and out of touch. We call his house number, but it does nothing but ring and ring. Calling Tyrone only confirms Curt is AWOL. Watching out the dining-room window, I am hoping my date doesn't call here again, asking when I'm going to pick her up. The last time she called, she advised that if I don't show up soon, she is going without me. As time clicks by, it is more evident I am more of a chauffeur than a date to my partner.

Finally, bright headlights shine in my eyes as a vehicle pulls up in our driveway. It is not the vehicle I expect. Instead, it is Curt's father's Transvan. The Transvan is a large van, bigger than a conversion van, with the amenities of a motor home. It has a couch, a dining-room table, and plenty of room. It will make the two-mile trip to the dance much more comfortable. The initial plan was to fit four in the backseat of the Pontiac, which would have been a tight but welcome squeeze on my first official date.

Curt explains that the Pontiac refuses to turn over, and he has spent the last two hours praying over it. Curt is a motor head, and if he can't get it to run, Jesus himself can't bring it back to life.

I sprint to the phone to catch my date before her angry mother takes her to the dance. After a quick conversation that involves a lot of phrases like "I am so sorry" and "Please forgive me," I sprint to the Transvan to pick up my date.

My date is the most uptight of the group. She is a sophomore, and it is also her first date. After I called her mother three weeks ago and asking if she could go, begging and pleading, she was given the green light to go. It is clear her mother doesn't like me much, but this is her daughter's first date, so she puts up with her daughter's ill-advised choice in dates. The tardiness of the night doesn't make me more likeable, and it is not helping me dig out of my unjust hole.

On the way to her house, it occurs to us all that driving up in a vehicle perfectly suited for making babies is not going to make my trek out of the hole any easier. It is a funny scenario until we pull up to her house.

I jump out, go to her door, and explain the situation. Her mother is not pleased, but because we are so late, she agrees to let her daughter go. The new suit, shoes, and corsage are what tip the scales, I am sure.

We arrive at the dance late, which works out great for me. We have less time to dance, and I am OK with that. After my date and I stand against the wall watching everyone else dance, the song "Angel" by Anita Baker pumps out through the large speakers, and my date twitches and can't stand still.

"Oh, this is my song," she says, and looks at me. Since the music is so loud, I pretend I can't hear her. We are not close enough as a couple for me to risk the embarrassment of getting on the dance floor. She turns to find someone else to dance with, and I am relieved.

The dance, or nondance, is finally over. I have survived without getting on the dance floor, and I am so happy. My date doesn't share my enthusiasm.

We all hang around and talk to friends and then make our way back to the Transvan. As we are walking, Jimmy Jam, a fellow track and cross-country teammate who is the best dancer in the school, notices my Roots.

"Hof, are you wearing Roots?"

I smile slightly and calmly and say, "Yeah."

"Nice shoes, Hof."

My reputation of being below average in the fashion department makes this a surprising and shocking sight to my friends. Inside I am busting. This night has been great, no matter what my date thinks.

We break up soon after the dance, after some female friends convince me I can do better. More and more I am becoming comfortable with myself. Finding my way and expanding my comfort zone become a journey with a reachable destination.

And the more time I spend with friends and their families, the
clearer that journey becomes.

The difference in food between my house and Curt and
Tyrone's house is shocking. One night while we're hanging out at
Curt's house, his mother asks if I would like to stay for dinner. Over
the past thirty minutes, I have sat in their kitchen and watched the
steam rise from the stove and create a tornado of smells twisting
and turning and spinning together. The tornado converges on
my nose, and a waterfall of saliva forms in my mouth.

I reply, "Thank you. Yes, I must stay…I mean I would love to
stay for dinner."

Curt's mom is making pepper steak, homemade rolls,
potatoes, sickeningly sweet red Kool-Aid, and peach cobbler for
dessert. I lean over and ask Curt who else is coming to dinner
and what the special occasion is. Curt laughs and tells me his
mom cooks like this all the time. She sets all the food out, and it
looks like a spread for a platoon.

Dinner is served, and I don't know where to begin. If I could
climb in this plate and bathe in this flavor, I would. The food is
spicy, hot, sharp, tender, and perfect. My mouth feels like it is
crying, sobbing, bawling for another forkful. The plate has my
undivided attention, and I completely block out the conversation
around me. All my senses are directed toward the end of my
fork. I eat until I can't eat anymore. I consider going into the
bathroom and trying to make myself puke to create more room
for more food. I decide against it because I am a loud puker, and
they will hear what I am doing.

The differences in my house and Curt and Tyrone's houses
are interesting. They spark an interest in me that I carry for years.
The differences in cultures fascinate me, and I enjoy pointing
them out. Faulting my parents for not going to school to learn
how to cook like a black woman from the South is not a thought
that invades my head. Yet, what I lack culturally, although it is no
one's fault, does create a small void in me.

Music is another area that is vastly different in my household
versus those of the kids I go to school with. Growing up, the music
we listened to was what Mom and Dad enjoyed: the soundtracks
to *Westside Story*, *Jesus Christ Superstar*, and *Godspell*; the music of

George Gershwin and Arthur Fiedler and the Boston Pops; the bands Simon and Garfunkel and Peter, Paul and Mary. Outside our front door on Whitcomb Street, the sounds of Motown dominated the air: the Jackson Five, the Temptations, the Four Tops, Marvin Gaye, Barry White, Aretha Franklin, and this Minnie Riperton woman were what my black friends listened to in their homes.

As I get older, the soundtrack from *Annie*, classical music, and ABBA are in our record player. Michael Jackson, Prince, the Time, and Run DMC are artists I share with my friends. I would never admit it publicly, but I like it all.

Mom and Dad take it too far when they drag us to orchestra concerts. I sit in the large theater at the Detroit Institute of Arts and wish for a national emergency, so I won't have to endure two hours of torture. To pass the time, at one concert (they take us to several), I hurl penny after penny into the crowd when Mom is lost in the music and not paying attention to what I am doing. *Peter and the Wolf* has never been so violent.

The dawning of my own interest in music really begins in the sixth grade. Stevie Wonder is adopted as my favorite artist. In school, I am introduced to Stevie's song "Sir Duke" from his album *Songs in the Key of Life*. I fall in love with the horns in this song, and Stevie inspires me. He becomes a hero of mine, and in music class, when we have to pick a musician for a report, I greedily snatch up Stevie Wonder. I go to the library and research anything and everything about Steveland Morris, a.k.a. Stevie Wonder. The report also has to include a song of the artist we choose. Mom purchases the entire album, which isn't cheap. It is a double album plus a bonus forty-five record. Timing shines on me, and I am allowed to purchase one of the best albums of the seventies.

Mom and I sit in the living room and put on the album, and we listen to Stevie together. I get lost in Stevie's poetry and his amazing blend of instruments. Mom likes how he speaks about injustice and is so politically aware. This is a special time for me, to sit on our old brown couch, listening to Stevie and sharing him with Mom. The music may not be her favorite, but the message and the fact that I like it mean a lot to her. In this music-filled afternoon, I learn it is all right to express myself and find my own way. It is an afternoon that will never depart from my memory.

Music becomes a way to express myself and bond to my culture. I am drawn to black artists, mostly R & B and rap. Becoming more aware of music helps me to assimilate with my peers. It is not forced or fake—it is what I grow to like. Having more in common with my peers makes me feel more a part of them. My only problem is that Stevie is my ground zero. The history of black music before Stevie isn't in my memory bank like it is with the black friends who grew up with it.

The loss of a culture is one of the things I grieve as a result of being adopted.

High school becomes a great training ground for learning how to socialize. I join the track team my freshman year and run all four years. I join the cross-country team my sophomore year and run cross-country my junior and senior years as well. Being a part of a team and getting to know people I otherwise wouldn't is a wonderful way for me to show others I am more than just the quiet, shy, little light-skinned boy.

Matthew also runs track and cross-country. He is the reason I join. Although we don't like to admit it, younger brothers do idolize their older brothers. James and Lisa have graduated by now.

I am sure high school is a totally different experience for Matthew, especially on the social side. Matthew is one of the only whites at the school. Our high school is accepting of our family, and Matthew is well liked. There are several black girls at school who find him attractive. Several times while he's walking down the halls, a black girl grabs his butt. I walk those same halls over and over and even a few extra times, and never once do I get a grab.

Matthew is very social and is able to function, as I am, in a black or white environment. He is at ease around blacks, and that gains him credibility and respect among blacks.

The conversations among blacks about whites are the same. The "us against them" mentality still rings loudly. At times, it makes me uncomfortable because it can be too generalized and very unforgiving. Never do I speak out against it, but I choose to disagree internally. Over time I understand the mentality is really more about a system than people. As we develop and mature we are able to understand that the "white system" is what oppresses, and not every white person.

As I watch others interact with my white brother, I learn something that makes me proud to be black. Although Matthew is a minority, he is given access and acceptance among my black peers. Although the talk is unforgiving when it comes to whites, if a white person is able to function with ease around blacks, that person is accepted. I deduce that because we, as blacks, have been the ones on the outside looking in, we are very tolerant and accepting when a white person makes the effort to be included. Matthew achieves this distinction and is often declared "a cool white dude," a very high title in our circle. This makes me proud of both Matthew and my black friends who let him into this circle.

This is how I perceive Matthew's experience in high school, but I am sure his experience as one of the few whites in a black high school has many challenges. I am not so naïve to think he just skips through his four years without any struggles. Again, I am certain he pays a higher cost in an environment where I am very comfortable.

For some it is a struggle, and they are not sure how to deal with our family. The racial combination makes them a little nervous. This usually comes out in conversations where several blacks and I are sitting around talking. One person says, "Then this white boy came up..." He stops midsentence. He looks up and then right at me and says, "Oh...no offense."

Again, I am not offended until he singles me out. It appears this same rule operates in the black community—the one that allows you to say something highly offensive as long as you say, "No offense," at some point.

The racial balance that we as a family try to find is still not an easy one. High school grows into a place where I am able to exhale and be comfortable, but the challenges are not completely erased.

In high school I learn not only more about myself but more about how people see my friends and me. High school is a lot like grade school. The student body is black, the teachers are white, and most of the schools we compete against are white.

Our high school has the reputation of being a very rowdy one. The members of the football team and track team have the reputation everywhere of being cocky. The football and track team members all wear black-and-white lettermen's jackets that have their nicknames stitched on the fronts and backs. They have names like "the Exterminator," "Bubba," "the Executioner," and "Dr. Doom."

Damon, a senior, adopts the nickname "Damian," the name of the devil in the very popular *Omen* movies. He has inscribed on the front of his jacket "Damian" and, underneath that, "666," the sign of the devil. To do this at a Catholic high school is a little over the top.

Being a member of the track team, I get to know a lot of these guys, and they are great guys—loud, boisterous, obnoxious guys, but decent guys. Their presentation of black makes me proud. Instead of blending into their surroundings, they are comfortable and confident in a skin that causes discomfort to so many. I adopt this lifestyle and become included with them.

Track becomes a large part of my high school experience and education. When the track team goes to invitational meets, which we do every Saturday from January to June, we are usually one of the only black schools present among a sea of schools. We give them "black" from the moment we step off the bus until the time we take home the first-place trophy. Our presentation of "black" is antiestablishment. If it is acceptable to be quiet and calm, we give them loud and crazy. By presenting ourselves in this way, we give the white schools that have very little contact with blacks a picture of "black" that is everything they expect.

Our sprinters dominate every event, and we give them every stereotype there is, and we are proud of it. Being teenagers, we don't see how damaging that can be. The team is lightning fast, and we blast the latest rap music from our bus. Several members of the team spend more time talking to women than running. Their aggressive style is harmless but terrifying to some of the rural white girls we compete against.

We are heard before we are seen. Mr. Mack, the head track coach and athletic director, and Father Pat, the distance and cross-country coach, struggle to keep the team out of trouble and focused. The superiority we feel is addictive. The power we possess fuels us. There is something intoxicating about dominating the white schools who we know don't like us. To be able to back up the talk, and in most cases be untouchable, is a nice feeling. In our minds, it is the polar opposite of society, so we cherish this feeling. Being superhuman is a great feeling, but it can be crushed in an instant.

The fall of my junior year, the Friday before homecoming, I arrive at school after Mom drops me off. Everybody is outside, gathered around the field house. The night before, someone spray-painted in large letters across the field house "Home of the Spear Chuckers." We are pretty confident that it has been done by some students from the white high school we will play in football the next day.

Mr. Mack tells us all to go to class, and I don't think much about it the rest of the day. After school, I change into my practice gear to begin another cross-country workout. The cross-country team stretches out in the parking lot in front of the field house, and this Friday is no different. We are stretching out and joking about the graffiti on the field house. Father Pat, our coach, hears us and shatters our calm stretching time as he yells, "That is not funny! That is how they see you!" The pain and frustration are all over his face. He tells us to finish stretching and go run. He does not tell us where or how far—he just tells us to go run. Father Pat, the only white in the group, walks off disgusted.

As we are running to nowhere, the gravity of the situation hits me. I understand what he is so upset about. It is the first time I comprehend the power of racism. To be viewed as something inferior and less than human, to be seen as savages, hits me hard. Racism that I have experienced to this point has rarely been so honest. I have often wrestled with the thoughts that I am either being too sensitive or too paranoid. Racism rarely confirms the intention behind the action. It leaves me to fill in the blanks.

In big letters spray-painted on *our* field house is how the suburban school views us. We don't have to connect the dots; we don't have to search for the hidden answer. It is the most defining, real, and devastating lesson I learn in high school.

Later in life, I learn just how much racism has affected our life as a family.

14

BLACKLISTED

While we run through the neighborhood playing games and being kids, my parents work to provide us with our comfortable way of life. Mom is the director of the Myasthenia Gravis Foundation, an organization created to support those afflicted with this debilitating neuromuscular disease. Her office is on the sixth floor in the old part of Mount Carmel Hospital on Outer Drive and Schafer in Detroit. The best part of Mom's job is the annual fundraiser. Each year, Mom sends out hundreds of three-by-five parchment cards to mostly athletes and people in the entertainment industry. The celebrities put on lipstick and kiss the three-by-five cards. The cards are autographed next to the kiss prints and sent back to be auctioned off to raise money for Myasthenia Gravis.

It is exciting to see the kiss prints arrive. I remember kiss prints from Jack Lemon, Ann-Margret, Charles Schulz, Grace Slick, Phyllis Diller, Brooke Shields, Lucille Ball, Danny Thomas, Jackie Gleason, Christie Brinkley, Gilda Radner, Jean Stapleton, Vincent Price, Ahmad Rashad, Rita Moreno, and Carol Burnett. The kiss prints are then put on display at a local shopping mall for a few days and then auctioned off.

One year, Mom returns home from the auction with a special gift for me. It is a kiss print of Gary Coleman. Gary Coleman plays Arnold Jackson on the TV series *Different Strokes*. He is the younger of the two black brothers who are adopted by Mr. Drummond, the wealthy white businessman. Arnold is the first famous adoptee I have ever seen. I am sure Mom understands the powerful significance of this gift, but I don't. The correlation between Gary Coleman's character and my life doesn't compute. I am too consumed with my life to be introspective at this age.

Dad remains the assistant to the bishop for three years. After the three years, the bishop's term expires, and he decides to accept a call to a church in Dayton, Ohio. The next bishop is a very close friend of the head pastor at the church in Dearborn, Dad's old boss. A career that had promise is brought to a halt with the placement of the new bishop.

Dad has to start looking for a new church to pastor. In order to interview for a pastor's position, it is required that the potential pastor have the recommendation of the local bishop. Before the present bishop officially steps down, he gives Dad the recommendations he needs to interview at some local churches. Hope has not totally disappeared, but it has a timer attached to it that is ticking fast. When the new bishop takes office, the needed recommendation will not be a given. In the months prior to the new bishop taking office, he confirms Dad's fear and lets the acting bishop know, "There is no room in Michigan for Pastor Hofmann." Dad will soon be shut out of all local Lutheran churches. The churches that are not local may grant Dad an interview, but it will be without the help of his own bishop. Many churches will want to know what kind of pastor Dad is, and they will logically go to his bishop to find out. Dad's career is crashing into the ceiling, and the timer is ticking louder and louder.

Dad receives an interview from a church in Warren, Michigan, a city not too far from Detroit. The church is in a racially diverse neighborhood, and Dad thinks this will be a nice fit.

During the interview process, Dad learns that the neighborhood surrounding the church is very diverse, but the church body is not. The existing members who go to the church have followed the white flight out of the city. The majority of the church members who used to live around the church have escaped to the white suburbs of Detroit.

On Sundays they make the trek back into Warren to have church because, unlike the members, the church building has not left. The church's lack of diversity and our family's obvious diversity is not a good match. After several interviews and Dad telling the church board of our unusual family, the church decides the parsonage that comes with the church will not be big enough for our family.

It is hard to believe there is a house smaller than the one we lived in on Whitcomb. They conclude that rather than inconvenience our family, they will not offer Dad the job. It is far worse to live cramped than to be unemployed—this is their conclusion.

Dad is granted an interview with a church in Indiana. The bishop in Indiana is a friend of Dad's and gladly parts with a recommendation. The church is located in Valparaiso, Indiana. Naturally, it would mean the family would have to move, but Dad feels being a pastor is what he is called to do.

For the initial interview, Dad is flown in to Indiana, and he meets with the church board. At the interview, Dad feels compelled to tell them about our family. As Dad reveals that it would take more than one color from the Crayola box to draw our family portrait, the interview turns from an interview about pastoring a church to an interview about who I am going to date.

By this time, I am in high school, and my choice of a girlfriend is a vital threat to the church and surrounding communities. Dad doesn't get a second interview, and he doesn't want one after this conversation.

Dad knows the bishop in charge of the Virginia territory, and he calls him to find out if there is a church in need of a pastor. The bishop follows procedure and recommends Dad for a position open in Richmond.

Once again, Dad boards a plane for an interview. Again, he feels honesty is the best way to handle our situation, and he explains to the board in the interview the construction of our family. Surprisingly, the board doesn't flinch. There are no uncomfortable questions or concerns. The interview ends, and Dad is excited. The interview has gone well with no hiccups. Before they proceed further, Dad requests that the board make the congregation aware of our family makeup. If they object, then we will know this isn't the church for us. The board assures Dad they will tell the congregation. Soon after returning home, Dad gets a call from the church in Richmond. They are very excited about Dad and want to move forward quickly. The church invites Dad back with Mom this time.

Mom and Dad are flown in to Richmond, Virginia. They are picked up from the airport and escorted by several members of the church board to tour some local neighborhoods and potential houses. Mom and Dad decide that a local neighborhood that is more diverse will suit us the best. After a frustrating ordeal, it appears Dad has landed a job and a way to feed his family.

Mom and Dad stay several days in Richmond and through the weekend. They attend church, where they sit and picture Dad in the pulpit giving his sermons. During church, Dad is introduced to the church body, and the excitement about a new pastor is evident. Immediately after church, there is a coffee hour held to allow the church to meet their new pastor. As Mom sips her tea and socializes with the church members, the subject of where we are going to live comes up. Mom explains that they like the diversity of a certain neighborhood and feel this neighborhood will be the best fit for our family. The church members surrounding Mom show their hand by the confused looks on their faces. Mom realizes the makeup of our family has not been explained to the church body. Feeling obligated, Mom explains.

By now, Mom and Dad know the effects such an unusual family can have on a church, so they make sure everyone is aware. Plus it is getting harder and harder to hide the little black kid on the end. Over tea, Mom explains the dynamics of our family. Nothing else is said about the conversation while Mom and Dad are visiting. They are taken to the airport later that afternoon, and the council tells them to expect a call during the week to finalize everything.

The phone never rings.

Expecting the worst, Dad finally calls, and his expectations are realized. The church leaders, who took Mom and Dad house shopping less than a week ago, have changed their minds. They are no longer interested in Dad being their head pastor. The job that seems like a slam dunk clangs off the rim loudly.

By now, the new bishop has taken over, and the old bishop's recommendation has expired. All the favors Dad has with other bishops have run out too. The ability to provide for his family is becoming narrower.

While Dad continues to look for a church, he finds a job as an interim pastor in Lima, Ohio, about two hours south of

Detroit. Dad packs up on Tuesday of each week and leaves early Wednesday to go to Lima to serve as a pastor, while the church looks for a full-time pastor. I get up for my paper route early Wednesday, and on my dresser each week is a note from Dad. In his distinctive, deceivingly neat but nearly illegible writing, Dad jots a short note to each of us kids. He tells us to have a good week and that he will see us on Sunday afternoon. Dad travels I-75 to and from Lima for about three months to stay busy and to get exposure, hoping this will lead to another church in need of a pastor. The lead never comes, and the need to get permanent employment is more pressing.

A position at a local hospital as the director of the Employee Assistance Program comes available. Dad went to University of Detroit and earned a master's degree in counseling many years age, which qualifies him for the hospital job. For the first time in a long time, he goes to an interview, and the racial makeup of his family does not dominate the conversation. In fact, it never comes up. Dad is hired quickly. It is not Dad's dream job, but it is a small sacrifice to maintain our family's way of life.

After about six years, due to hospital cutbacks, they slash Dad's salary by $10,000. I hear Mom and Dad talking about it and how hard it is going to be for us, and I get that same sick feeling in my stomach that I had the weeks that followed the purse-snatching incident.

Dad endures the job at the hospital until, two years later, they cut the job completely. Dad decides to sell life insurance instead of going through more disappointing interviews with closed-minded churches.

I am never privy to any of this while it happens. Mom and Dad never share the stories of the disappointing interviews while they are happening. While in high school, I am never aware that we almost move to Richmond, Virginia.

I am aware of the changes in jobs but just assume every now and then adults change jobs. The only job change that affects me is when we move to Shaftsbury, and that is a great and needed change. All the other changes and the dynamics behind I find out about as I interview Mom and Dad for this book.

Mom and Dad do a great job of shielding me from all of the ugliness that they face. I walk through a lot of it not even noticing what is going on around me. I walk through it all not realizing the stress Mom and Dad are feeling. It isn't until I am in my late twenties that it occurs to me that my parents have bad days, they get sick, and they bleed if they get cut. As I sit down to write this book and begin talking to Mom and Dad about our unique situation, the events that have gone on around me come out. More stories of adversity come out in between my games of baseball and Ditch It.

Dad tells a story about us going camping when I was about three years old.

He and I walk up to the office to rent a site to camp. The owner looks at Dad, and he looks at me, and he refuses to rent us a spot. He says they are all filled, but looking at the campground, it is obvious there are several spots available. We turn and walk away, and Dad realizes there isn't much he can do. We get back in the car and drive to the next campground, where we are welcomed without any questions.

Mom tells me the story of us going to see some old friends from Dearborn, a fellow pastor and his family. We are camping near their new home in Wisconsin and put them on our itinerary. Our friends have family visiting from out of town when we are in town. Their extended family is not as open minded as our friends, so in order to visit, they have to come see us at the campground. Painfully, while sitting at a weathered picnic table, the pastor admits I would not be welcomed by the extended family.

It is every parent's desire to shield his or her children from the ugliness of the world. Mom and Dad are handed shovel after shovel of ugly, and I never know about it. The sacrifices they make for me are never recognized until the ordeals are small memories in the rearview mirror. These recurring stories of prejudice, whether blatant or subtle, occur around me, but not to me. Mom and Dad spread their parental wings over me and protect me from the ugly. Knowing all of these events are direct results of my presence would cripple me. Instead, this knowledge falls on their shoulders, and I continue my games of baseball and Ditch It without knowing the pain and struggle they endure.

As an adult, I am again humbled, hearing story after story of how unjustly our family was treated. In my head I wonder if their extreme decision to adopt me was too costly. At every turn it seems the family is affected by my presence. I am grateful, but I am not sure if I am worth the high price they paid. My parents will say it is all worth it, but this is something I must ponder. Their protecting me from all this is far beyond amazing.

Unfortunately, the microscopic particles of hate occasionally seep through, and I return the favor by shielding Mom and Dad.

15

MY FIRST

Vocabulary Lesson One

Black
A crayon or a stick of licorice

Oreo
One small, black, round cookie
Sweet white filling
One small, black, round cookie

Coon
A furry, black-masked animal

Spear Chucker
A primitive hunter

Jungle Bunny
An exotic rabbit

Spook
A tiny ghost-like creature

Porch Monkey
A small primate who inhabits a porch

Every year my family and I go on vacation. It is usually for a week or two in the summer. All six of us and Trixie, the family collie, pile into our car. The pop-up camper is attached to the car, and we drive to our destination.

My mother is the ultimate planner, and every minute is accounted for. On day one, we drive six hours and stop off at the KOA campground five miles off the freeway. We set up camp, enjoy the campground for two and half days, and then pack up and head to the next destination. This is the type of itinerary we follow. Included in the itinerary are stops to the local towns to get food and stock up.

There is one trip to the local grocery store when I am eight years old that I will never forget.

The six of us arrive at the grocery store. Trixie stays back at the campground, attached to the camper by her leash. In the car on the way, we are given the traditional preshopping schedule. We are told there is a shopping list, and we will not deviate from it. No extras, no add-ons, no treats. The car rolls into the parking lot, and the mission is about to begin. As soon as Dad puts the car in park, we all spill out. Mom is the commander in chief, and she is focused on getting everything on the list cheaper than anyone else has in the history of mankind. To say money is tight for a family of six on a Lutheran minister's salary is the biggest understatement in the history of mankind.

To Mom's credit, no one has every stretched a dollar like she does. Somehow the elastic in our dollars are stretched farther than the elastic on Dad's Fruit of the Looms. We descend upon the grocery store like a Green Beret unit. Mom is in charge of getting us out alive with the budget still breathing. As mission commander, Mom has no respect for the honor code, "No one gets left behind." There are many incidents where she turns a corner and disappears into the produce section, leaving us kids to wonder where she's gone. Sometimes, she fakes one way, sees a sale on canned goods, and goes another, and leaves the four kids dumbfounded. If we aren't careful, someone is leaving the store with a fractured ankle. Her moves can snap an ankle like a twig.

Dad is never stressed. He is like an old war dog. He is very familiar with the drill and able to track Mom through the store. Oftentimes he is gone for several minutes but picks up Mom's scent in baked goods and falls right back in line. It probably isn't too hard to find a family with four children who loathe the food-reconnaissance missions like we do. We have no reservations about voicing our displeasure.

On this particular mission, we walk around the grocery store for what feels like hours. As we shop, we keep crossing the path of a white family who has a boy about my age, seven or eight. I manage to keep one eye on Mom and one eye on him. We see each other at the end of an aisle or a few aisles over, and we make eye contact. We start making faces at each other, and this game goes on for the majority of our marathon bargain hunt. I see him and stick out my tongue, and then he sees me and pushes his nose up like a pig's. Or I give him the thumbs-up, and he returns with the thumbs-down. This is a great way to distract me from the grueling task of comparing prices.

Finally, we complete our mission. We have gotten the best prices on corn, hamburger, hot dogs, baked beans, paper plates, plastic forks, and aluminum foil. There is no way we could have gotten a better deal unless we stole the corn and a pig from a nearby farm and ate it with our bare hands.

Quickly, we pay, and it is time to rendezvous back at the Hofmann vehicle. This is when the traditional dance begins between my parents and us kids. This store has the gumball and worthless-trinket machines in the front-entrance area, and just outside the store are small penny rides. There is a horse and a car calling my name as they sit idle.

I know the rules; I can't make an audible request for money. If I want candy, gum, or a ride, I realize the price of that will have to be multiplied by four, and there is no way we are going to ruin the vacation by blowing the money we just saved on such luxuries as candy, gum, or a horse that slowly moves up and down for one minute. But the kid in me has to at least try. I slow down and look longingly at the beautiful multicolored gum and candy. Then I look back at Mom and then Dad. My face lights up with a smile at the possibility of getting a coveted piece of gum. It has never worked up to this point, but the hope sends adrenaline through my body. Maybe today my cunning plan will work. My parents know the routine, and they pretend not see me. I try to slow the caravan, but there is no use—they keep on walking past the gumball machines.

This time I have an idea. I will run up ahead to the rides—this way I will have more time to really give them an Oscar-winning performance. There should be no way I will be denied.

As I run up ahead, I notice my friend from the store is riding the horse. Here is my chance—my acting ability combined with another kid whose parents obviously love him enough to let him ride. I know I am golden.

As I am waiting for just the right time to give my parents my look, I stroll by the boy on the plastic hollow steed. He is selling the ride. He has on jeans, cowboy boots, and a T-shirt and is riding the horse like it is a wild mustang. This is my first chance to see him up close. I want to impress him, so I go for the sure thing. I am a big fan of the TV show *Happy Days* and think the Fonz is the coolest man on the planet. I stroll by my friend and give him my best Arthur Fonzerelli impression, complete with both thumbs up and a "Heeeeeeey." He looks down at me with a half smile that seems more evil and sinister than friendly.

"Nigger!" he says softly.

He knows my parents are too far behind to hear him, and his parents are nowhere in sight. Suddenly the importance of riding the horse vanishes, and I am changed. Time is paused. This boy who I thought was my friend is really the opposite. In an instant I realize the playing that we were doing in the store was not friendly on his part. He was antagonizing me. I just never got close enough to him in the store to realize it.

The utterance of that word steals life from me. I go from being an eight-year-old kid on vacation to a small and black kid in an environment that has very few people like me. That word takes me immediately to a place where I am alone and different.

Until now, I haven't noticed that in this small rural town, I haven't seen one other black person the whole time we have been here. I feel like I have lost with no way to win at this playful-turned-evil game we play. This mature realization floods my mind all in a matter of one step. I am certain in that one step that my whole demeanor changes and part of my childhood innocence is assassinated. Defeated, I walk away and never mention to my parents what happened. I shield them from the ugliness.

I still picture the expression on his face. He is proud and convinced he is superior. He is so convincing that *I* believe it.

In this instant, I learn that this word is a very powerful word, a word that has no rebuttal. There is no other word in the English language that can conjure up so much emotion. It is a word that always frustrates me. When a white person says that to you, no matter what you say back, there is no word as demeaning, degrading, and devaluing as "nigger."

I do not consider myself a violent person, but I know if a white person were to call me a nigger today, I would feel justified to respond with a possessed rage that would make the Tyson-Holyfield ear-biting incident look rational and understandable.

In the late sixties and early seventies, "nigger" was used more frequently. Today the word has been changed from "nigger" to "the 'N' word." It is understood that it is not a word to be used openly. Even typing the whole word makes me uncomfortable.

Growing up it is a weapon. Soon after my first "nigger," I begin to hear it more and more. It is like the whole world has discovered "nigger" the same day I have. I realize my sensitivity is heightened to the word, which makes me more aware of it.

My brothers begin to use it. It becomes their first weapon of choice when we are arguing, and I have no response. My best response is to pretend it doesn't affect me. Mom, Dad, and Lisa never use the word, and I am never concerned that that is a possibility with them.

My brothers use it for its effect rather than its meaning. As preteenagers, they have no idea of the gravity of the word. In the heat of battle, you use the most lethal weapon. You don't stop to analyze the social and moral aspects of using it. I mention this to some of my friends who are black, and they are appalled. I don't put that much weight in it when it comes from my brothers. Do I really think they mean it? No, they are attacking my weak point and doing what they can to win a fight. As we get older, they grow to understand the word and use it less and less.

In high school, I find out we are like most families. There are certain things you can say about family, but no one outside the family gets that same privilege. That is how it is with us.

An incident occurs in high school that I will never let vanish from my memory. The incident occurs during my junior year, involves Matthew, who is a senior at the time, and has a profound effect on me.

Even though we've had our differences growing up, Matthew is my best friend, especially in our early years. Because we are so close in age, we are each other's playmate. I also think that, because we are such an unusual family, there is comfort in each other. When I am the minority, because of his experiences, he understands what I am going through. When he is the minority, I understand too. Matthew and I extend this friendship as we become teammates on the track and cross-country teams in high school.

My junior year, I injure my leg and spend the majority of track season rehabbing from my injury.

Initially, even though I am injured, I go to the meets and cheer my team on. After a while, it is too depressing to go. To sit and watch people win races that I know I could if I were healthy is more painful than my injury. I choose to stay home and work at rehabbing my leg instead of watching this torture.

One Thursday, as I head home, the track team assembles and competes against another local Catholic high school. Our high school has become a powerhouse in track, and this meet should be very uneventful. Again, the competition is the same—our mostly black school against a mostly white school. Although the competition on the track will not be much, the meeting of an all-black school and an all-white school in Detroit often makes the uneventful eventful.

The team we face on that Thursday has one runner I know very well, Eugene Crampfish. He has become my number-one rival and was the only one to beat me at the state-cross country meet last fall. He is a wiry white kid who is about five feet six and 130 pounds, and he has a mouth that moves several seconds before his brain.

At this particular track meet, something happens between Eugene and my brother Matthew. My friend Derrick Louis calls me later that night and gives me a play-by-play of the incident.

Derrick doesn't know how it started, but all of a sudden, across the track, he could hear Matthew screaming at Eugene. Everyone ran toward the shouting, hoping to see a fight. Matthew and Eugene were yelling back and forth, and as Derrick got closer, he could hear they were arguing about *me*, and Matthew was defending *me*!

Then Eugene said something under his breath that only Matthew could hear, and Matthew lost it. All rational thought and behavior left Matthew. He charged at Eugene, and from everyone's account, it was obvious Matthew was going to kill Eugene right on the infield of the track. Several coaches, including Father Pat, our distance coach, jumped in between them, more for Eugene's safety than anything else. Normally, once Father Pat got involved, that was the end of it. That Thursday it didn't matter. Matthew could not see or hear Father Pat through the red clouding his vision and the alarms going off in his head.

Matthew kept charging after Eugene, pushing past Father Pat. Some of our teammates tried to pull Matthew away and calm him down, but it didn't work. Matthew was determined to separate Eugene's head from his body.

Eugene was conflicted. There was a strange chemical reaction going on in his body. His testosterone was telling him to stay there and fight, but his adrenaline was screaming, "Run, Eugene, run!" He didn't know which signal was more rational. Matthew's storm of fury confused Eugene. Eugene hadn't counted on this volcanic reaction. Instead, the chemical reaction froze his brain, and he stood there in a catatonic state. Eugene wasn't sure what this crazy white boy was going to do to him, and his posture showed that Eugene didn't want to find out. He made sure there were plenty of people between him and Matthew.

Eventually, Mr. Mack, our head track coach and school disciplinarian, stepped in to save Eugene's life. Mr. Mack is feared by *everybody*. He is a stocky five-feet-eight white man with horn-rimmed glasses and a brush cut, and no one has ever stood up to him. His loud bark would immediately cause whatever is in your bladder to sprint out.

When he stepped in, Derrick reports, the confrontation was defused, and rational thought immediately returned to Matthew. Matthew was sent to the team bus and not allowed to compete that day.

My imagination convinces me Eugene called me a nigger. After all, one white guy calling a black guy a nigger in front of another white guy—who's gonna say anything? Who's it gonna hurt?

Eugene made a similar mistake during a basketball game last season. He called one of our players a nigger, and Eugene's nose has been crooked ever since. His mouth still works way ahead of his brain. He probably assumed on the track that the lonely white guy on our team would not object to the "N" word. Eugene didn't figure the lonely white guy was my brother.

What Matthew did that day was very risky. He risked being tagged as the "crazy white boy." Interestingly enough, that moment of mindless rage earned Matthew a lot of respect from my friends at school. They all saw it as Matthew just trying to neutralize an enemy who deserved to be neutralized.

In the end, it doesn't matter to me what was said or how it looked. All I know is that my big brother stood up for me. Matthew never says anything about the track meet when he gets home, and after talking to Derrick that night, I never ask Matthew about it.

We still fight after this, but the word takes another hiatus, only to return one last time a few years later.

We are both home on spring break at the end of my first year of college. Matthew has brought his girlfriend with him. We have gotten into it again (over what, I don't know specifically). Matthew is trying to still prove he is the big brother. We are yelling back and forth, and I am not backing down as I usually do. My first year at college has been a racial awakening, and I am sick and tired of being treated like a second-class citizen at college and refuse to be treated like it at home. Matthew is frustrated with the fact that the fight is not going as easily as usual and resorts to calling in an air strike. Matthew begins to shout at me, in front of his girlfriend, "You ni…" He never gets the full word out.

I lunge at Matthew and push him into the grandfather clock made by our grandfather for my mother, which sits in the corner of the foyer. I am prepared to put him through it if I have to. To my surprise, Matthew doesn't fight back. This is shocking because growing up Matthew was a fighter, a scrapper. This time, he backs off and looks at me like all rational thought and behavior has left me.

The grandfather clock clangs and shakes from side to side. This violent noise brings Dad out of his upstairs office. Dad storms down the steps in what seems like one quick motion and ends up between Matthew and me.

Dad has rarely gotten involved in disciplining us as that is part of Commander Mom's responsibilities, so whenever he does get involved, we know it is in our best interest to quit doing whatever we are doing.

"What is going on? What is this about?" Dad demands.

Matthew and I both respond in unison, "Nothing."

The fight ends there in front of the swinging, bonging grandfather clock. Once again I don't feel Dad needs to hear about this ugly word that has crept into our house over and over again.

The relationship Matthew and I have changes that day and that moment. The verbal and physical battles stop. We come to a place of mutual respect and admiration that we couldn't have gotten to without something like that happening. The word is buried, and Matthew finally understands from my reaction the gravity of that word.

The utterance of this one word is not as damaging as the silence I have allowed around it. Growing up, I think if I ignore how this word makes me feel, I can eliminate its effect on me. My poor attempt to combat hate and violence with silence fails. Instead I give much more power to this word and the incidents attached to it.

I am often asked if I would change anything regarding the way I was raised, and for many years I would quickly say no.

As I put my thoughts to this page, I have a first and last regret. I regret that we didn't talk much about race or its effects on us in our home. We were destined to be affected by it, and ignoring it only gave it power it didn't deserve. Since we didn't openly talk about race, I would go on to make decisions without the knowledge of how race could affect those decisions.

16

DECISIONS

The starter's pistol shatters the silent November air. The one hundred of us who qualify for the state cross-country meet take off. This is my senior year and my last high school cross-country race. The ground of the golf course shakes as we head toward the first turn. Two hundred yards into the race, I look around and find that I am tied for last place. I look to my right, and there is Mike. We are numbers ninety-nine and one hundred.

The rest of the runners are ahead of us, but instinctively we don't panic. We look at each other and then around us, and I say, "OK, let's go get 'em, one at a time." We pick up our pace but realize this is a three-mile race; there's no need to sprint at this point. Slowly, one by one, we move up. We stay side by side for the first mile, passing one overexcited runner after another. Mike is a sophomore, so to be at the state meet is an honor. There are very few sophomores running this course today.

We both continue to move up but now at a different pace. We lose each other in the large crowd, and my eyes concentrate on the back of the head of the runner in front of me. I tell myself over and over again, "One at a time. One at a time." It is a trick I have learned. I try to concentrate on anything but what my body feels. I try to trick my body into just moving forward. I ignore my lungs, which are screaming, "Slow down—we need more air." I am coming off a bad injury from last spring and am not expected to qualify for the state meet.

Father Pat, my coach, for the first time doesn't tell me where he expects me to finish. He knows I have lost a lot of valuable training time trying to heal. My cardiovascular fitness is not where it needs to be to compete in a race like this. Father Pat just tells me to run well. I am in the race now, and my competiveness wants to prove to Father Pat that I can do well. Father Pat mentioned to me just before the race that if I finish in the top ten, he will be surprised. I have no idea what to expect or where I should finish. I only know each person I pass gets me closer to the finish line.

Since I started out the race so far behind, I have no idea how far ahead the leaders are in the race. The only thing I can do is "one at a time."

Once I pass one, I look ahead to the next head I must focus in on. I look *ahead* fifty yards to the next head. I train my eyes to focus on how his hair moves with each step. I hear and see nothing else but his hair flopping up and down. I also concentrate on my breathing. I breathe in rhythm with my strides, and this takes my mind off the lack of oxygen.

I am one of the only blacks in the race, and that motivates me to do better. To do well in a sport that is dominated by whites gives me a passion to do better than I am expected to do. The "us versus them" mentality in a strange way motivates me to prove I am just as good as the white runners.

One by one, I continue to move up. As I pass each runner, I look for any signs of weakness. I look for heavy breathing or an awkward stride. My feet touch the grass without sound. As I pass other runners, I hold my breath. This has to look effortless and easy. I pick up the pace for the next twenty to twenty-five yards. I do not want them to go with me, so I have to pass them quickly.

I continue up and down the rolling hills of the golf course. Some hills are as steep as forty-five degrees, and I use them to crush the spirit of any runner around me. Sprinting up a hill, I pass a few more who are struggling to make it to the top. At the top of the hill, out of earshot, I gasp for air and recover.

Constantly and methodically, I move through the course until I can see what looks like heaven, the finish line.

The finish line is now four hundred yards away. This gives me energy, and I see three or four people within striking distance. I set out for the first one. As I pass him, he tries to go with me. I know I have to beat him now to make sure he doesn't come back closer to the finish. I usually wait for the last one hundred yards to begin my sprint, but I can't afford to have this runner hang with me. He picks up his pace, and I pick up mine. He is still there, and I have to shake him, *now*!

The sooner I leave him, the sooner I can slow down to recover before my last sprint to the finish.

He will not back off, and now it is a battle of who will give in first. I increase my pace, and so does he. We are stride for stride, and I am running out of room. This game has taken up one hundred yards, and I have got to dispose of him now. I decided that if he is going to beat me, I will drain him of all his energy to do so. I begin to sprint, breathing in and out, still in rhythm, as if I am in labor. My lungs are about to explode, but I have to finish him. I swing my arms back farther and lengthen my stride. He drops back one step and then two, and I feel him surrender. The fracturing of his will makes a distinct noise. I have broken him.

He will not come back, but my energy is depleted. The two or three runners that I had a chance at, I can't get. I am running on fumes. The next one hundred yards I use to recover. I expand my chest to take in as much air as possible; I need to fill my lungs. As I do, I listen. The fear of footsteps behind me is distracting. I listen, and I hear nothing. To turn around and look is a sign of fear and weakness, and if someone is in striking distance, he or she will consume me. I watch the fans who have lined the last one hundred yards to the finish, and their eyes are on me and not behind me, which tells me there is no one close to me.

It is time to go again, up on my toes and go, time to leave every ounce of energy on this cold golf course. I begin to pick up the pace, and within twenty yards, I am at a full sprint. The finish line races toward me, and I lean in across it.

Now I can feed my lungs the air they have been craving.

Father Pat meets me just beyond the finish line, and I just want to hear the number ten. He is excited and asks, "Do you know what place you got?"

I am still panting and feeding my lungs. I squeeze out, "No."

He hugs me and picks me off my feet. "You got fifth!"

The energy I lost over the last three miles comes flooding back to me. The top seven get the distinction of all-state honors. I passed ninety-five people, and I am all-state for the second year.

I got it right.

My performance gets me noticed by colleges, and I begin getting letters and phone calls from some colleges and universities. One day while I'm sitting around the house, the phone rings. There is a loud and excited man on the other end. He asks for me, and he explains he is from a small private college up north, Alma College. I have never heard of the college before, but I don't tell him that information. He introduces himself as Coach Charles Gray, the cross-country and distance coach for the college. He tells me to keep up the good work and congratulates me on my success. I hang up the phone and am excited some college would call to talk to me.

Over the next few months, I don't hear much from anyone. I get information in the mail from several colleges and really don't give anyone much thought. I enjoy my high school experience and am not looking forward to leaving. Over the past four years, I have gotten very comfortable with myself and my place in high school. I am not part of the popular crowd, but I am not part of the crowd everyone ignores either.

My athletic ability has grabbed attention and made me moderately popular. Running track has saved my life socially. My success in track and cross-country has given me confidence and the opportunity to allow people to get to know me. Because my high school is such a small school, the confidence I gain in running gives me the courage to be more social. I am a long way from the closed-off freshman I was four years ago.

Winter indoor track begins, and we flow quickly into regular track. I have trained hard over the off-season, and I am ready to end my high school track career with success. As we begin track, the rumors of our track team being state champs starts right away. The year before, while I was injured and sitting at home, our track team went to the state meet and returned home state champs. I pray I can complete this track season injury free.

I do well throughout the season, being moderately successful along the way. As we enter April, we begin to prepare for the important meets, and my competitiveness forces me to train hard. One day while practicing, I notice a pain in my right foot. I ignore it, hoping it will go away. It doesn't and stays with me for two weeks. The nagging pain forces to mention it to my coach. This is only after he notices me limping.

Father Pat acts immediately. He calls a friend who is a doctor, and we drive thirty minutes to nowhere, and the doctor examines my foot and takes x-rays, all free of charge. Father Pat uses the priest thing to his advantage and does a great job of talking people into anything. In minutes, the doctor is back to show us an invisible crack in one of the bones of my foot. I have a stress fracture, and although I can't see it on the x-ray, I can see the rest of my season quickly fading away.

Resigned, I am ready to leave, but Father Pat is not ready to give up so quickly. He asks the doctor what we can do. The doctor states he has a friend who can design a shoe to protect my foot.

We go see the friend, who is also a foot doctor, and he confiscates my running shoes. We return a few days later. He has installed in the soles of my shoes steel rods to adsorb the impact and protect my feet. He has to put them in both shoes because they add a noticeable amount of weight to the shoes, and running with only one weighted shoe would throw off my stride. We take my new heavy shoes, and we leave. The redesigning of my shoe cannot have been cheap, but I never see a bill. Father Pat works his priestly magic again, or he pays for it and doesn't tell me.

I practice with the shoes, and soon the pain is gone, and I am back on schedule.

We arrive at the regional meet; I finish both the mile and two mile in first place and qualify for the state meet.

Coach Gray from the small private college calls later that same night.

"Hi, Coach—yes, I ran well today. I qualified for the state meet in the mile and two-mile races."

I hold the phone away from my ear as Coach Gray lets out an excited cackle. "What place did you get?" he asks.

"I finished first in both," I proudly state.

Habit causes me to back away from the phone again. When he calms down he tells me he will be at the state meet to watch me run. He wishes me good luck and ends the conversation.

I wait two weeks for the state meet to get here, and I am nervous and excited. I love to compete in these races. The distance races are always dominated by tall, skinny white kids. When I was just starting to run well my junior year, I loved to look down the starting line and see that I was the shortest and the darkest of all the runners. I am sure they never counted me as their competition.

Our school is known for their sprinters. We are always thought to be one of the best track teams in the state because of our sprinters and relay teams.

The state meet is my chance to show in the white-dominated events that blacks can compete with them too. The racial pride that I adopted in grade school has grown to inspire and motivate me.

The team arrives in Jackson, Michigan, the night before to prepare for the meet. We get our room assignments, and then the sprinters, the shot-putter, and I meet out by the pool. It is not the pool that attracts us, but the girls' track team from Benton Harbor who has congregated there. Some couple up and disappear, but most stay and just talk. I meet a sprinter, and she is surprised to know I run distance. She is even more surprised when my coach comes down with the program of tomorrow's meet. It has the times of each runner from his or her regional races. As we expect, our sprinters and relays have run the fastest or second fastest in most events. My mile and two-mile times are the fastest for both races. I am the one to beat in both of my events. Coach could not have come at a more perfect time. I can see in this young lady's face that she is impressed.

Coach announces loudly that we have to go get dinner. He pulls us away from our new friends. Father Pat believes girls make you run slower, so he does what he can to break us all apart. We return to our rooms to get ready for dinner and to break up one couple who found their way to one of the beds. This sprinter isn't only fast on his feet.

We go to dinner, and my excited stomach won't allow me to eat much. We discuss our chances at being repeat champions, and our chances are good. A high school from Flint that seems to always have a strong team is still strong, and it appears we will compete with them for the championship. Flint is also strong in the sprints. They do not have any distance runners with them. Father Pat comments that I may be the difference between first and second place tomorrow. The pressure inspires me.

We return to our hotel rooms, and Father Pat is in for a long night. He stations himself in the hall outside our hotel rooms.

He stands guard, so no one can leave or come in, mainly the girls' track team we met before.

We call back and forth to the girls' rooms, and we devise a plan. We tell them to come over but come around to the back of the room, the balcony side. Father Pat stations us on the second floor, making it more difficult to escape. The girls are standing below our balcony, and we let down a bedsheet. One by one our shot-putter pulls them up.

We sit and joke for hours with the girls, and then we lower them down, and they go back to their room. One of our sprinters wants to go back with them, so we lower him down too. We all go to bed at about 3:00 a.m. Then the phone rings. Our sprinter has been caught in the girls' room. Their coach is now walking the hallway to make sure they don't escape. For the next hour the quarantined sprinter calls to our room over and over again. He finally escapes and makes it back to our room. At about 4:00 a.m., we get to sleep.

At 7:30 a.m. Father Pat pounds on our door and tells us to be ready in thirty minutes to go to breakfast. We meet at the van at 8:00 a.m.

Shortly after breakfast, we arrive at the track, which is decked out, ready to host a state meet. We all scatter to prepare for our races and events. I have plenty of time, so I go and find the friend I met last night, and we walk around most of the day. My mind is not on the races.

I have a routine to prepare for my races. I usually go to bed about 10:00 p.m. the night before, visualize each lap of each race, memorize my split times for each lap, pray, and go to sleep. At meets, before each of my races, I go over each race again. I stretch out, warm up, and get ready to race. Today is much different. I am functioning on very little sleep, and I am too distracted by this cute sprinter to go through the races.

As I am walking around and doing some stretching, I see several college coaches who know me. They are the coaches from Eastern Michigan University, Western Michigan University, Siena Heights College, and Spring Arbor College. They all wish me luck. Coach Gray runs up to me and hugs me and is much more excited in person. He wishes me luck and tells me he will talk to me later.

I am too busy laughing and flirting with my sprinter friend to notice my race is about to start. Father Pat hunts me down and yells for me to report in on the track. I do so, and we start the mile race.

The race starts fast, and again I know not to panic. I then try to shift into second gear, and nothing happens. I try to concentrate on the head in front of me, but I can't focus. I try to pick up the pace, but as I do, those in front of me do too. Then they do the unexpected. They start to pull away from me, and I can do nothing to hold on. The race finishes well before I do. I end up in eighth place and manage to secure a medal and one point for the team. My brain is fried, and I don't know why.

I return to the stands and talk things over with Father Pat. We agree the mile is over, and I must prepare for the two mile.

The two mile, which is usually the race I do better in, goes even worse than the mile. My energy and focus are gone, and I do good just to finish. I do not finish in the top eight, so I get no medal and no points for the team.

I return to the stands, and Father Pat consoles me. I feel terrible, and all the coaches who spoke to me earlier just look at me and don't say a word. I retreat down the steps to go get my sweats, and I meet up with my sprinter friend. She consoles me by giving me an unexpected hug.

We walk around the track, and a sprinter from River Rouge High School runs up to me and points at me. "Man, I lost some duckets on you. What happened?" I just walk away. There are other black schools like River Rouge that I have seen all year, and they also enjoy watching a short black kid beat the tall white kids.

The sprinters have done well all day. They keep us in the hunt for the championship. After my race, Father Pat totals up our score, and although the meet isn't over, we determine it is impossible for us to win. We take second. We lose to the high school from Flint by eight points. I was expected to bring in twenty points, and I have brought in one. Father Pat was right. The championship has come down to me. It will take me years to get over this failure.

My close friends Derrick Louis, Greg James, and Steve Butler have driven up to watch me run, and I decide to ride back home with them. The ride back in the van would not be a pleasant one with the sprinters. As I am leaving Coach Gray stops me. "Well, today just wasn't your day. We would still love to see ya running for us." We shake hands, and he says he will call me.

Later that summer, my parents drop me off at Alma College in Alma, Michigan to begin my college career. My decision is based on the fact that Coach Gray has never given up on me. I ignore the fact that the student body at the college is 99 percent white and in the middle of cornfields. I never discuss or consider how I will fit in, in an environment that is all white, all the time.

17

OPPRESSION

The door to my small dorm room closes, and the sound bounces off the empty walls. Mom and Dad just hugged me and said good-bye, and I sit on my small bed alone. My new bed is about 150 miles north of Detroit at a private Presbyterian college. I am trying to rationalize in my head why I chose to come here. The academic answer is to study exercise physiology so I can become a physical therapist, but my question is far beyond the academic answer. This college is the whitest place I have ever seen. The student body is about 1,100 students, and of those 1,100, I will soon find out thirteen are black and mostly from the Detroit area. What did I agree too?

As I walk across campus and take classes, I realize how unique Detroit is. Although I live in a neighborhood that is predominately white, everywhere I go in Detroit, I see black people. Detroit is my protected bubble. I don't have to go far to be part of a majority. My white in Detroit was really tan. This college white is blinding. Detroit has shielded me from living as a true minority.

College gives a more realistic view of America. I now live among people who do not understand what being black is like. I am shocked to learn at a freshmen gathering that there are some in my new community who have never seen a black person in real life. The closest some have come to a black person is watching them on TV. In 1985 there are still very few positive portrayals of blacks on TV.

I resent that, and a confusing anger boils in me. I realize that for some, exposure to another race is optional. For minorities, it is unavoidable. The fact that some can carry out their lives without ever having to come in contact with any other cultures causes my anger to always simmer just below boiling temperatures. The luxury of having this choice (a choice I have never and will never have) makes me mad.

As lopsided as Detroit is racially, I could never go a day without seeing a white person. The knowledge that there are some cities where there are no blacks and that those cities can get along without blacks hits me hard. They have no need for people like me, and I feel that as I walk to class.

I feel powerless because my section of this new population has no voice. What I find even more infuriating is that those of us who have this common bond can't get along. I find there are some blacks who do not wish to associate with other blacks. I guess they think if they are seen with us, people will realize they too are black. I quickly write them off as sellouts and kick them out of my community. Surprisingly, they don't need us, and they function fine without us.

My first week of my freshman year, as I am walking out of my dorm, I see a dark-skinned black student. He right away comes up to me and starts a conversation. I am starved for the human contact that I am used to. We strike a bond right away. He is from Brooklyn, New York. He is Jamaican, so his Brooklyn-Jamaican accent right away makes him interesting. His name is Lindley, and sophomore year we become roommates. We both joke about how we landed in the middle of white America coming from two of the blackest cities in America. We keep each other afloat as we tread through these foreign waters. We virtually cut off all the other blacks because of their lack of blackness, their desire to associate more with the white population than the black population. Actually, I am not sure if we cut them off first or vice versa.

The other blacks are more mainstream and put on the disguise of being white, and Lindley and I have no desire to do so.

Our dorm room is our fortress of solitude. We stay up until all times of the night laughing about how crazy this white place is to us. Because we feel like a contagious disease, we don our blackness to the highest degree. We give them every stereotype they expect. We are loud, rude, and mean. We sport do-rags and African medallions, and oftentimes our speech is incomprehensible to those around us. Our slang is as thick as we can make it. It is our way of keeping them at a distance.

Needless to say we don't fit in very well, and our egos tell us it's OK.

This is the first time in my life I feel what oppression is like. This system is so unfairly weighted that I have no chance at winning. To speak up and complain is seen as weak, and I will be labeled too sensitive. Instead, I learn to say nothing.

One evening, I am in my dorm room, lying on my bed, studying. A group of my cross-country teammates has been drinking, and they pass by my room. My door is slightly open, and as my teammates walk by, they see me and spill into my room. A white student who makes the mistake of thinking we are closer than we actually are jumps on top of me and pins me down. His freckled face is inches from mine as he sits on my chest, and I can't move. He puts his finger on my nose and loudly states, "You're black!" He laughs loudly, and the others with him do not know what to do. I hear silence broken with nervous laughter, and slowly they all pour out of my room. I am left feeling helpless and ashamed— ashamed that I did not decapitate him right there. That feeling that I came to know so well growing up quickly comes back. Now everyone knows it. I am different again.

For the next few weeks at cross-country practice I am very cold toward my freckled-faced teammate. He notices something is wrong and confronts *me* about *my* attitude. He clearly remembers the incident, and our versions of the story are identical. He can't understand why I am so upset. My feelings are dismissed, and his conscience writes it off as me being too sensitive. This new life is a crazy mirror image of the life I am used to, and what I see as clearly wrong is somehow justified as right.

It is this tilted justice and my awareness of it day after day that wear on me. It is not as obvious as someone shouting "nigger" at me every day, but the effects are the same. It is how I am treated differently on a daily basis that crushes my self-esteem.

When a white person who I am friendly with greets his white friends with "hi" and greets me with "what's up," I feel that difference like a coat that is too small wrapped around me. When a white friend shakes the hand of another white friend and offers me a high five or grabs my hand and wrestles with it in his attempt to give his version of a black handshake, I am again shoved in the box, set apart from everyone else.

When I come around the corner in my dorm, and I hear someone giving his imitation of what a black person sounds like, and he immediately stops when he sees me, I feel like an outcast. Every conversation I have with a white student could involve some unconscious or conscious slip of the tongue that directs all the attention to me, and that makes me want to pull away. I resolve that if I'm going to be seen as different, it will be on my terms, not theirs.

I realize now, twenty years after my four-year sentence at this college, that I still can't write about these experiences without anger and frustration seeping through my pen. The incidents continue as I feel all eyes are watching my every move.

One afternoon, Lindley, a black girl from Detroit, Todd, a white friend from our hall, and I go in to town. On our way back from grocery shopping, we notice a bunch of milk crates behind the grocery store in an alley. We pull over and fill the car with the crates, thinking they will make great additions to our rooms. We each take three or four crates and return to our dorms. Within fifteen minutes, the police are at our door. Someone saw us taking the crates and called the police. They got Todd's license-plate number, and the police traced it back to his dad, who happened to be a professor at the college. The interesting things is that the police showed up at our door first, not Todd's. Somewhere the police had to inquire about two black students and were directed to our room. The police tell us to call everyone involved to our room, and once everyone arrives, the police collect the crates and lecture us on how bad it is to steal. Lindley and I don't consider this stealing. If you leave something like this out behind a store in an alley in Detroit or New York, it is trash.

When this story is told as an isolated incident, it is easy to see the misunderstanding, and many will argue this is all it was— just a misunderstanding. It would be hard for me to prove them wrong. So I am left to ponder if it is me or if it is them. Am I too sensitive? Am I the crazy one? Am I looking at life through a lens that needs to be corrected? It causes me to question myself. It causes me to question my actions. It causes me to be afraid to take another step for fear I will step into another "misunderstanding."

I have inherited my dad's affliction. Every situation now has the potential to be racial.

While I am at this small private college, the atmosphere is not overtly hostile. I am not aware of any groups gathering to talk about white supremacy. There is never a time where I am attacked because I am black. But the environment is not openly welcoming. It is obvious to me the college doesn't know how to address these subtle issues, so they ignore them, which makes me feel ignored. The fact that I have only one other person who sees things as I do is maddening.

Dating in college is a new experience. I joke that I am an equal-opportunity employer, stating I will date any race as long as she looks good. My sophomore year I date my first white girl, a girl from Naperville, Illinois. Prior to us going out, I meet her parents. They are presidents of the parents' association. They are quirky folks but a lot of fun. Everyone loves them. They are very active around the college and visit often. They show up at Halloween, and her father is dressed as a cheerleader, and her mother is dressed as a football player. They make the rounds through all the dorms, trick-or-treating, and even go to some of the frat parties. They are seen as the coolest parents at the college.

The spring following their Halloween appearance, I begin dating their daughter. She is goofy, silly, and a little smothering, but she helps my four-year sentence at college pass. She is more into us than I am, and she can't wait to tell her parents about us.

She calls me over to her room one night, and she is in tears, sobbing uncontrollably. Through her sobs she tells me she has told her parents about us. As she calms down, she notices she is getting no comfort from me. She goes on to explain to me how they took the news. Her father could do nothing but sit at the kitchen table and cry. Her mother said nothing. Her silence sends a strong message. This is heartbreaking to see my potential presence in their family has caused these likeable people to be so unlikeable.

A few weeks later, it is parents' weekend, and we are still dating. My enthusiasm for the relationship has waned, but it is better than spending time alone. Her mother is still not talking and refuses to come to parents' weekend despite the fact that she and her husband are head of the group sponsoring the weekend.

She can't bear to see her daughter with a black boy. Her father comes, and I refuse to meet him.

I have to work in the cafeteria as part of my financial-aid package and to survive. As I am working, she and her father walk into the cafeteria, and our eyes meet. He makes a weak attempt at being friendly, and I picture this man sitting at a kitchen table weeping. My respect for him is gone, and I make no attempt at all. I walk by him as if he is not there.

My temporary girlfriend is heartbroken, and I am annoyed. She goes to talk to a campus counselor, and the counselor requests that I come back with her. This is the weight that tilts the relationship-work scale. This relationship is too much work, and I do not care to devote that kind of energy into this insanity. I end the relationship and pity their family.

My junior year, I meet a girl from Grand Rapids, Michigan. She went to a more diverse high school, and through our conversations, I can tell she is more comfortable around blacks. She sells me on the "my best friend at home is black" argument. She is nice and attractive, and again time goes by quicker with company. She grew up with her mother, who was a single parent, and her growing up was a struggle. She is not part of the privileged group that dominates this campus. We date for about six months, and on a break from school, she asks me to come home and meet her mother. As we pull into the driveway, the phone in the house rings. The girl's grandfather, who lives nearby, has been in a car accident. He and his wife are at the hospital but will soon be released and taken home stiff and sore.

We turn around and head to their house, about thirty minutes away. In thirty minutes, I get to meet the entire family, including an uncle whom my date has told me fought in Vietnam, is half crazy, and hates black people because of something that happened between him and some black soldiers in Vietnam. I also get to meet an aunt who is liberal minded and I am told will like me.

We arrive at her grandfather's home. Soon he arrives with a bruised and bandaged forehead, and all the kids and grandkids trip over each other to show their concern. He is not a warm grandfather at all. They all cater to him to stay in his favor. They are all afraid of him, and he controls the family in a scary kind of way.

We are introduced, and he extends a hand that is limp and fish-like. I shake it, and he says nothing to me. Instinctively, I want to pull out my family portrait and show him I have some ties to white people, but I quickly accept that there is nothing I can do that will make him like me.

I meet the uncle, the war veteran, and I cut the conversation short. My fear is I will say or do something that will cause him to flash back to Vietnam, and he will begin spitting out racial slurs that could make a trucker blush.

I meet the aunt, and she is friendly, and I direct all my attention to her and my girlfriend, when she isn't catering to her grandfather's every need. My girlfriend is noticeably one of her grandfather's favorites, but our being together does not hold his attention or get his blessing. I stare at the second hand on the wall clock, willing it to move faster, while praying to God this uncomfortable meeting will end soon.

We continue to date for over a year, and some at college are all right with it, and some of her friends are noticeably uncomfortable with us. Several of her friends spend their time whispering in her ear, telling her she can do better than me. They are on constant watch, just waiting for me to prove them right. Their hatred for me is unfounded but very aggressive, and I am constantly retracing my steps to see what it is that I did to set them off. While in the middle of this character assassination, the obvious escapes me.

I am still learning the many faces of racism and bias, and oftentimes racism is cloaked so well it takes me a while to recognize. In many cases I don't see because I am not trained yet to see, and I don't want that to be the answer. I am hopeful that people will see beyond my skin tone, but just as I am not trained to spot bias, many are not trained to look past it.

There are times when it seems like things are coming at me from all sides, so I make sure to keep my circle of friends small to cut down on the collateral damage. My circle is contained to Lindley and whomever I am dating at the time. Soon that circle gets even smaller.

Early in my junior year, Lindley announces that he will be graduating a semester early. I have been regretting him leaving already because he is a year older than me, and it means I will be alone on campus for an entire year. Now with him leaving early, this means my alone time is stretched to a year and a half.

In preparation and out of sheer panic, I search for a new social network. My only other good friend on campus is a fellow Detroiter named Carl. He grew up in a neighborhood that butted up against my neighborhood and went to the one of Detroit's toughest high schools, Henry Ford. Carl is a year younger than me, tall with chocolate-colored skin, and kind. I didn't know Carl in Detroit but was familiar with his older brother, who was a popular DJ around Detroit.

At college Carl is an active member of one of the fraternities on campus, and I have a lot of acquaintances in the same fraternity. I have never considered being in a fraternity, but I think, "Why not?" since this is the group I feel most comfortable around. It's funny, but comfort is considered in degrees. The thought of being totally comfortable is abandoned, and I am comfortable accepting the next-best thing, finding the group less likely to call me a nigger. I know it is never a guarantee, but among Carl's fraternity, I feel less likely to be called a nigger.

To this point I have never considered the Greek life because there are no black fraternities on campus, and several of the fraternities make it clear they aren't open to having any black brothers in their groups. I also am aware that going home and telling my black friend I joined a fraternity that wasn't a black fraternity is going to be met with a look—the look that says I went to this white school and am turning white and away from black. But now I have no choice. I have to do something to make the next eighteen months go by quicker.

Every fall pledging for fraternities and sororities begins after rush week with a big ceremony on Friday night called Run Outs. The whole campus congregates in the gym, and each fraternity is positioned in different areas on the gym floor. All the pledges stand on the gym floor, and one by one each pledge's name is announced, and he runs to the group he will soon call his brothers. I have watched this ceremony take place several times, and the sport of it is trying to figure out who will go where, although it isn't really that difficult. Each frat has a particular style and reputation, so it isn't hard matching student to fraternity.

There is the Theta Chi fraternity, the students who like to smoke weed, the burnouts. There are the TKEs, the athletes who rule the campus in property destruction after a night of drinking— basically the football team with Greek letters. The Sigma Chi fraternity has the reputation of being very anti-anything that isn't white. I have several friends whom I knew and associated with prior to them pledging Sigma Chi. After they pledged, they cut off all contact with me and all other people of color.

One year the Sigma Chi fraternity decides to dress up special for the Run Outs. They arrive at the ceremony and walk into the gym single file, dressed in white jumpsuits with hoods. I sit in the stands, and a chill goes through my body. Their resemblance to the KKK as they stand silent with the white hoods pulled over their heads is eerie. In my mind this is no mistake. These are bright kids who know what their reputation is, and yet they still choose to show up dressed like the sons of the grand wizard. I don't know what is more frustrating—the fact that they feel comfortable doing it or that no one questions it, takes exception to it, or challenges it.

The last fraternity is the Sigma Alpha Epsilons, or the SAEs. They are the richer white kids who seem to be the most tolerant of people of color. As I said, my black friend is a member, and they have two Indian brothers who are high-ranking members in the fraternity, so they are more open to diversity than any other fraternity. This is really my only option.

In the fall of my junior year, I stand in the dance studio below the gym and look at the envelope marked with my name. The studio is the holding pen for hopeful pledges prior to the Run Outs. In the envelopes are the bids. If a fraternity wants you, they place a card in your envelope. It is possible to have four cards or no cards in your envelope. I slowly open my envelope, hoping for one and only one card, hoping to see the letters SAE. My heart is using my rib cage as a conga drum. Everyone I have talked to told me I would be getting a bid, but in these few seconds, I wonder if maybe they are playing a cruel joke on me, and the envelope will be empty. I slowly tear into it, and to my relief, there is a bid from the brothers of SAE. I look around the room, watch other people open their envelopes, and wonder what bids they got. After we have all opened our envelopes, we're told to get in a line. We will be escorted up the stairs to the gym, where we will declare which frat we will be pledging. As I get in line I notice a few hopeful pledges exiting out of the dance studio through the rear door. Their envelopes are empty.

I think what a horrible process this is and how sad it is that we just all want to be accepted and liked. Too often there are people who just don't fit in anywhere. My heart goes out to those few students because that is how I feel so often on that campus.

I wonder what those who didn't get a bid will do tonight, and I feel their loneliness.

We enter the gym, and the crowd goes crazy. I am one of about twenty-five pledges ready to declare our allegiance. One by one we step forward and tell the MC our names, and he loudly announces us to the crowd. Then the soon-to-be pledge runs to the group of his choice.

I am in the middle of the line, and I stand and watch as student after student unveils whom he will be brothers with. I am nervous and excited and wonder how I got here.

Most students are dressed in jeans or sweatpants. I am dressed in wool pants, a leather sweater, a wool sweater, and a large leather three-quarter-length jacket. My Roots shoes are still cover my feet. I have learned that I may not have the wallet size of most students, but coming from Detroit, I have inherited some understanding of fashion. No one is as clean as me tonight. No one is as hot as me either. What possesses me to wear that much leather and wool at one time I do not know.

Finally, it is my turn. I tell the MC my name, and he announces me. I slowly unzip my jacket and casually walk over to a group of girls from the SAE sister sorority, hand them my jacket, and pull from an inside pocket a dark blue T-shirt that has the yellow letters of SAE. I hold it high above my head, turn, and sprint to the group of waiting brothers. The gym rocks and shakes, and I jump into the crowd of screaming frat boys, and they lift me high above their heads and carry me around. For a brief moment, I feel accepted. I feel a part of something. But that is all it is…a brief moment.

The night ends with a party at the fraternity house, and people who have never spoken to me before speak to me and congratulate me and hug me. Girls I don't know want to dance with me and get close to me. I think to myself, "OK, this is what college is like in the movies." The night ends with me and Chris, the only other student who decided to pledge SAE, standing in the middle of the large party room at the fraternity house. We are each given a large beer stein. They know I don't drink, so mine is filled with water. Chris is a drinker, and his has been filled from the nearby keg. They toast us and then instruct us to down the contents of our steins as the room cheers us on. I guzzle it down and think to myself, "How in the world could someone do this with alcohol?" I am drowning in the water. We finish our beverages, and the crowd closes in around us, welcoming us to the family.

I leave the party in the early morning and am told to return to the house the next afternoon. I do as I'm told. All the brothers have assembled in the meeting room in the basement, and we are escorted in. The room is dark except for a few candles, the leaders of the group are dressed in ceremonial robes, and the mood is much different from the night before. It is businesslike and very solemn. My new pledge brother and I are brought to the front of the room and told to bend over and look straight ahead. We are instructed that our fraternity fathers are behind us and will be welcoming us into the family with a ceremonial swat with a large wooden paddle. We are not allowed to turn around until after the swat to see who our fathers are. The members begin to cheer and egg on the swatters. Several times I hear them tell the swatters not to go easy on us. We are told to prepare, and they count off: "One, two…"

"Wait!" someone yells. "You guys better grab your jewels, so they don't get in the way."

Chris and I grab our testicles and pull them forward so they don't get squashed by the paddle.

The counting begins again: "One, two…"

At "three" I see white, white pain unlike anything I've ever felt before. It shoots from my butt to every last one of my nerves. It takes my breath away. The room erupts with cheers and laughter, and I begin to wonder if I've made a mistake. Once my breath comes back, I turn around to see Carl behind me. He is my fraternity father and the one who struck me.

Now that the party is over, the hazing begins, and it is nothing too serious. It is mostly people telling us what to do and treating us like crap, and we have to take it. The orders and the disrespect touch a nerve, and I can't shake the added weight that comes with rich white kids telling me what to do. Some really get into it, and they become different from the people I thought they were. This goes on for two weeks. The disrespect combined with the lack of sleep that comes from early-morning assignments take a toll on me. This is all on top of the twenty hours a week I'm working in the cafeteria and a class load that is challenging due to my prior education not preparing me too well for college.

Each time I am called to the house and ordered to do some degrading task tilts the scales in a negative direction. I understand that the goal is to break me down to build me up, but the end game is becoming less attractive. I keep thinking that after six weeks of this treatment, I am going to hate everyone attached to this fraternity, and then I'll be stuck with them.

The final straw comes during my second week. I have been advised that in a few weeks my pledge brother, Chris, and I will be responsible for taking several members off campus to a party. The bill for their food and alcohol will be split between Chris and me. This is also the time someone tells me about the fraternity dues that I will owe at the end of this humiliating process. The scales tip even more. I am a struggling college student, and my small paychecks are gone most of the time before I get them. I decide it is best I return to my solitude and de-pledge from the frat.

I concentrate on studying, working in the cafeteria, and spending time with my girlfriend. It all makes this sentence go by quicker.

As I inch closer to graduation, I realize I will be leaving soon and fantasize about the black women I will meet when I go back to Detroit. I'm concerned about how my black friends back in Detroit will receive me when they hear I am dating a white girl. In anticipation of this fantasy and in fear of ridicule, I end the relationship for no legitimate reason. In the end, I decide interracial relationships are too much work. I am not strong enough to wage the war and prove to the world why interracial relationships are all right, and I don't have the desire to fight the world every time we go out.

College is a bitter but necessary experience for me. It is like swallowing medicine that tastes like dirt. The act of forcing the medicine down is painful, but digesting the medicine will make my future more tolerable. I am given a huge dose of the real world, and it is overwhelming. The loss of control is devastating. In Detroit, I was a part-time minority. I knew when and where to expect to be treated differently. At college, I am a minority every day, all day. I miss those who are like me, those who understand me. I also miss the likeable me. This change in environment is such a shock to my system that my personality changes, and I become someone *I* don't even like.

Throughout my four years, I do make several white friends, and their companionship is welcomed. The shame is that I could make so many more good friends, but I make it impossible to see them over my self-constructed wall. The struggle for me is identifying who the right ones are to let in and how to keep the wrong ones out. I am convinced those I do get to know have the potential to betray me behind closed doors with racist remarks and attitudes. Moving through college is like walking through a minefield, scared that my next step could end in an explosion I will never hear. This fear creates a lonely four years. The confusing part is that this fear is sometimes accurate and oftentimes just my own paranoia.

I regret that the shade of black that I choose to show is the shade so many of my white friends have seen on TV and in the movies. The shade of black I regret not showing is a shade that's unexpected. The shades with tones and hues that show more than what society markets are what I should show. I choose to protect myself and shut down, cheating everyone around me. At this age, I don't have the energy to speak for an entire race.

My tutelage in the "us versus them" mentality saves me. Instead of taking on the burden that it is I who am deficient, I understand from this mentality that it is "them." The pride in my race props me up and allows me to withstand the exclusion and oppression. This pride protects my outer shell, but my internal wounds do not heal so quickly. I manage to survive, but some inner gashes leave scars that I am still nursing.

Experiencing this environment bonds me to those heroes in the past that endured much more. Prior to college, real oppression was in a textbook that had no feeling attached to it. Going through it and its invisible effects strengthens me.

College helps me to understand the sacrifices that Mom and Dad made to protect me from this realization earlier in my life. Although it is a shock to my system, it comes at a time where I am mature enough to handle it. The four-year degree I receive in real life becomes more valuable than the bachelor's degree I receive in the spring of 1989. This is not the only priceless lesson I learn while at college.

18

MOTHER?

Are you my mother?

There is a children's book written by P.D. Eastman called *Are You My Mother?* It is the story of a little bird that hatches when his mother is away from the nest. The bird then sets out to find his mother. He goes up to animal after animal and simply asks, "Are you my mother?"

Off and on I feel like that bird. I want to walk up to women and just ask, "Are you my mother?" It is my fantasy that after a few negative responses, I will find my mother, and she will deliver a worm to me and hug me just like the mother bird does to the baby bird in the book.

Growing up I always wondered about my biological mother. The thoughts of wonder led to fantasies about my mother being rich and her coming to find me. I'd imagine that when she located me, she'd give me a big basket full of money. She'd then leave me with Mom and Dad but check up on me every now and then to drop off a new basket of money each time.

If she isn't rich, she is famous. I imagine I am the descendant of royalty. British royalty or Hollywood royalty, it doesn't matter. Then I wonder what I would sound like with a British accent or how I would look in a big Hollywood mansion. My stream of consciousness takes me on a wild ride down a river that eventually arrives on the opposite side of the earth, far away from mother thoughts.

My mother thoughts never leave me, but they do not consume me either. On special occasions like Christmas or my birthday, I wonder if she is out there and what she is thinking about. The emotions I have for her are hard to describe. I do not miss her because I never had her. It is more of a haunting curiosity. My vivid imagination soars through time and space occasionally, hovering over her to just watch how she interacts with and moves through life. The thought of being close but invisible is soothing. Direct interaction is terrifying.

In college I decide to venture out and see if I can find my mother. The solitude of college gives me the courage to try to stitch together fantasy and reality.

Through the phone I can hear her leaf through the pages of my file. She gives very short answers to my long questions. The most common answer I get is, "I'm sorry—I can't tell you that."

On the other end of the phone is the woman from the private adoption agency. I sit at my desk in my dorm room and picture my file. I imagine it to be three to four inches thick and pregnant with papers, notes, reports, and information about me. It is often said people go away to college to find themselves, and I am attempting to do just that.

Being away from home, I realize the sacrifices Mom and Dad have made for me, and it heightens the sense of family and closeness I have for them. This idea of family makes we wonder about my birth parents and the circumstances that caused them to give me up for adoption. The wonder is concentrated on my birth mother. For reasons I can't explain, my father is of some interest, but my mother is the treasure I seek.

My fantasy continues about the woman who created me, what she is like now, and what she was like when she gave me up. I hesitate to pursue her because I am not sure her reality will match my fantasy.

I am also hesitant because I don't want Mom and Dad to feel slighted. The urge to protect them and their feelings is very powerful, and part of me thinks if I go looking for my birth parents I will somehow betray the ones who have loved me unconditionally.

I call home to Mom and Dad. I tell them how college is going, and for the first time ever I ask questions about my adoption. I hold my breath as I ask what agency handled it.

The research I have done to this point tells me that this is the first place to start my journey. On the other end of the phone, Mom and Dad explode. It is like they have just been waiting for me to ask. They download to me years and years of information and give me the name of the private adoption agency. They explain to me the circumstances around my adoption and anything they can remember. I hang up the phone relieved, and I am certain they do too.

The next day I place a call to the adoption agency in Detroit. I am transferred to the woman assigned to my file. I give her my name and birth date, and she asks me to hold on. I imagine her going to a large filing cabinet and pulling out my file. She returns to the phone, and I begin to ask questions about my birth parents. The shuffling of paper begins. She tells me that my birth mother did not sign a consent form. The consent form would allow me access to the file the caseworker holds in her hands. Since there is no consent form in the file, my access is denied. This frustrates me because technically my birth mother did not say I could *not* see the information. She never said either way, but since this one piece of paper is not in the file, my birth mother's right to privacy trumps my right to my own information.

This thought plays over and over in my head. I am sitting at my desk in the corner of my dorm room, and I am talking to a woman in Detroit. She, who has no connection to me, knows more about me than I do. The names of my birth parents, and their social security numbers, are all on a desk in Detroit, and I can't see it. I sit at college powerless. There is no arguing this, and it appears my search has ended before it begins.

As a consolation, the woman informs me that she can send me my "nonidentifying information." She explains this is information about my birth parents that is just that, nonidentifying. I want to scream and yell and chew this woman's head off. She is only doing her job, but I want to flood her ear with the injustice that I feel about this system. Fortunately, my rational side knows she doesn't have the power to do anything different. The phrase "a bird in the hand, a bird in the hand" rings in my head.

I resign myself to giving her my address at school, ask her politely to send me what she can, and thank her for her assistance.

An eternity passes over the next two weeks, and I wait for the paperwork to come. Finally, it arrives. I open the envelope, and there in seconds, I learn more about myself than I have ever known.

I am the son of a white woman and black man. He was a cook, and she was a cafeteria worker. They worked at one of the major auto companies in Detroit. They were married, but to other people.

This is a screwball I did not see coming. I have always assumed they were two young kids who got caught in the moment. The fact that I was the result of an affair is shocking. Over the years, my imagination filled in the blanks, and I was not even close. I painted the picture of two teenagers who had me and then went their separate ways.

The idea of having brothers and sisters was never drawn up in the sketch I'd created of my birth family. In these two pages I find out I have three brothers and one sister from my birth mother's marriage. My birth father also had children, but it doesn't say how many. They were both still married at the time of my birth; neither planned to leave his or her spouse.

My creative mind imagines the conversation my birth mother had with her husband about me, and I am sure it was a colorful one.

This information is the least I learn. The conversation I have had with myself over the years about these two strangers and who they are surprises me. I have always assumed I was not giving it much thought, but seeing my reactions to the truth tells me I put a lot of thought into it.

My interest again is concentrated on my birth mother. I learn she is five feet one and was just over one hundred pounds when I was born. She has blond hair and blue eyes; that makes me laugh. I am the son of a blond and blue-eyed woman—again, not what I pictured. I want to see what she looks likes, hear how she sounds, see if any of her mannerisms were passed on to me. For the first time I realize a foreign thought. There is someone out there who looks like me. After years of being the different one, I comprehend that there is someone who shares my DNA.

My creative mind continues to digest this new information and begins writing a new script. My story is now that my birth mother has me and continues living. The children are too young to remember, and her husband ignores this bump in the road but never forgets. The auto-company rendezvous and the resulting pregnancy are never mentioned again. I fade away like a bad phase my birth mother went through. To her, I am out of sight, out of mind.

Since I can't connect with those who know the truth, I make it up. The desire is still in me to get the full truth from those who created me. I want to know why I was put up for adoption, and I want to know the real story behind the standard answer I've heard all my life: "Your mother couldn't take care of you and wanted you to have a better life."

I have never known what that is supposed to mean.

The letter is folded, and I store it with my memory book Mom gave me when I graduated from high school. I call Mom and Dad, and I tell them what the letter says, and they are excited to hear about what we never knew. They are happy that I got to fill in some of the blanks. Dad encourages me to try and find my birth mother. I tell him my search has come to a roadblock. I have received all the information I am allowed.

Dad tells me to look her up by her last name in the phone book. I feel like I am having a conversation with a child. "Dad, they will not give me her name. That is part of the identifying information I don't have access to."

Dad responds: "On your original birth certificate, I think you were listed as 'baby boy Pervine.' There can't be a whole lot of Pervines in Detroit."

I am shocked. Now I have a last name that I either didn't hear or that was left out in our first adoption conversation. Dad says it like everyone knows it. "Wasn't that it?" he says to Mom, who is on the other phone in the house.

"Yes, I think you're right."

It is not much, but it gives a faint heartbeat to my search. The next day, I make a call back to the adoption agency. My caseworker grabs my file, and again I hear the maddening turning of paper. I ask her if she can tell me my birth mother's name. Before I finish the sentence, I know her answer: "I am sorry—I cannot give you that information." We have been through this before, and I am sure she has been through this with many, many adoptees. She is so rehearsed in it that she can say it with if no feeling or compassion at all.

The conversation goes quiet between us, and I am searching my mind to get any more information out of her. I blurt out, "My parents told me her last name is Pervine. How do you spell that?" Desperation is intertwined with my words, and the conversation goes quiet. She has turned down the temperature of her cold heart. She is just not going to answer my question.

After a few more seconds, she says very professionally, "As per our earlier conversation, I cannot give you that information." I don't respond. She repeats what she just said. "As *per* our earlier conversation, I cannot give you that information."

She is giving me a clue, and I am missing it. My desperation has thawed her heart. "So it is P-E-R-V-I-N-E, right?"

Quietly she says, "Yes. Is there anything else I can help you with?"

"Nope, that is it. Thank you very much." I hang up the phone.

I search for "Pervine" in the Detroit area and don't have any luck. The desire to find out more surprisingly and quickly subsides. The idea of busting into a family that probably knows nothing about me is not very appealing. The fact that I now have a last name satisfies my immediate appetite. I end my search with some blanks filled in and with a new story with a more realistic explanation.

My search does not end with a worm and a hug, but I am satisfied. The memory book that holds my information is packed away, and the urgency to dig for my lost treasure is replaced by the need to digest what I have learned. In the back corner of my mind, I occasionally pick up this information and toss it around. Periodically, I toy with the idea and hope that somewhere in the Detroit area, there is a blond-haired and blue-eyed woman who is searching for me—and that my story of being gone and forgotten is not close to the truth.

For now fantasy replaces reality again, and I am satisfied, but the possibility of what I might find or who might find me is exciting.

19

HOME AGAIN?

In May of 1989, I leave college, grateful for the mind-expanding experience and more grateful it is now over.

My studies in college have gone well despite the fact that I chose and stayed with the wrong major. I entered college with the hopes of becoming a physical therapist and majored in exercise physiology. Chemistry class and genetics class very quickly killed that hope. I struggled with the course work in my major but breezed through the course work in my minor, English. During my senior year, it occurred to me that I probably should have majored in English. Fortunately, I did well enough to secure an internship at St. Joseph Hospital in Ann Arbor, Michigan, with their cardiac rehabilitation department. Although this was not my initial goal, it is a chance at a viable career.

My plan is to go home to Mom and Dad in Ohio, where they have landed finally with a church that Dad pastors in a small rural town. It is interesting what door opens once the black kid is away at college. I will spend the summer there and then leave to go to Ann Arbor to start my internship in the fall.

A small town and my newfound independence don't mix well. The leap from Detroit to this rural town is painful. I have finally been paroled from college/prison, and this small town doesn't have the excitement I need. Again I struggle with making new friends, and the black population is close to nonexistent in this little farm town.

The shift from being on my own to under my parents' roof is stifling. We have all enjoyed our freedom the last four years, and I can't go back to "My rules, my house." I spend two or three weeks with my parents and realize I have got to go for the betterment of the family and my sanity.

I place a call to Detroit, to Mrs. Tenbusch, my best friend's mom, who lived across the street from us on Shaftsbury Street. I ask if I can stay there until my fall internship begins. I am welcomed back, just as I expect. I inherit John's room, which is now empty as John has stayed in Chicago after graduating from college. Mike and Mollie are away at college, and Joey, who has grown up to become Joe, is the last child at home.

To this point, I have had a decent relationship with Joe. He is six years younger than me, so as I grew up I did not spend too much time with him. He is a friend by association through Mike.

Joe is now fifteen and submersed in high school. We spend the summer together playing basketball and lifting weights in between my work schedule. Joe is a respectful, quiet, and thoughtful fifteen-year-old who is on the verge of finding his comfortable place in teenage life.

We sit in the basement watching rap videos and playing video games hour after hour and talking about everything and nothing. Joe is a scholar when it comes to the civil rights movement. He knows far more than I do about great black leaders and Detroit's history. I adopt Joe as the younger brother I never had or wanted, and I cherish our new friendship.

Jose is still living next door with his mom while he attends a local college in the Detroit area. Mr. Galano passed away while I was at college. The bitter taste and thoughts I had for Mr. Galano were totally dissolved well before Mr. Galano died. Over the years, the Galanos have become part of my extended family.

It is good to be home, blasting the radio set to WJLB, the biggest black radio station in Detroit, and playing basketball with these two guys who transformed into brothers over the years. No longer do I have to question the intentions of those around me. Once again, I breathe in calm and allow myself to relax. I fit in again, even though I am surrounded by white people. I can just be me, and finding this place at this time of my life is priceless.

During this summer, I can't find a steady job, so I hire on as a "Kelly girl" with Kelly Temporary Services. The lack of funds easily washes away pride. I spend May and most of June doing temp jobs in and around Detroit. I quickly learn I can't do this for too much longer.

In mid-June, I learn the internship I thought started in September starts in two weeks, and I have no place to stay in Ann Arbor. I extend my stay with the Tenbuschs through December and commute to St. Joseph's, which is forty-five minutes away.

The internship is my first exposure to the real workforce. I shadow the cardiac technicians who run the cardiac-rehab classes for those fresh from cardiac surgery. I also watch and assist with stress tests. Soon I learn this really isn't my type of work. As I watch the cardiac technicians set up, administer, and complete the stress tests, running up to twelve in one hour, I realize the scales are uneven. They are paid not much more than minimum wage, and the cardiologist who sticks his head in occasionally gets paid a six-figure salary. I grow to detest the cardiologists, who are very pompous and condescending to everyone. The internship clearly teaches me what I *don't* want to grow up to be in life.

My first exposure to adult work life is an easy transition. College has prepared me well, so I expect to be the only black where I work, and it is not a shock when my expectations are met. The anger and bitterness that I had in college don't follow me home or to work, and I am able to function and socialize easily. The comfort of knowing I can retreat to Shaftsbury Street at the end of the day, where I am understood, creates a happier me.

Playing the work game comes easily. I quickly realize I must function differently at work than I do at home. Thanks to all of my growing pains, this can be done like the flip of a switch. I know to talk proper while at work (finally, talking proper has its advantages). I know to present myself at work more polished and articulately. When I exit work, on the ride home I can blast my rap music and relax. While with my friends, I strap on my tongue that speaks slang and talk in a way that would be incomprehensible at work. This double life is a necessary part of functioning in the work world and a priceless gift to comprehend. I know many black friends who are unable to switch back and forth, and success in the work world is impossible for many unless they flip the switch. If I had understood the need to do so in college, I would have fared much better.

In December as my internship ends, I send my résumé out and begin looking for a job. My plan is to stay in Detroit, the city that is such a comfort to me. I search and search, and I can't find a job. I return as a Kelly girl just to have *some* money.

I know it is time to move on and out of the Tenbusch basement. Mrs. T. would let me stay there forever, but it is time to try and fly on my own. I only need a decent job to support me, and I can find nothing.

One day when there is no temporary work, I go down to the MESC (Michigan Employment Security Commission) office. This is a service to help the unemployed find employment. I go and stand in a line that wraps around the outside of the building, wearing my shirt and tie and carrying a handful of résumés. Finally inside the building, I am directed to a line to register. I wait in that line, fill out the necessary paperwork, and follow a pointing finger to another line. In this line, I wait to take some kind of test. This test will help me determine what kind of job I should be doing. After I finish the test, I am allowed to sit down and wait for an employment professional to call my name, so we can discuss my future.

I sit in the back of the room and look around. Despair descends on me like fog. There are professionals in suits, young mothers with small children, and blue-collar workers in working-man coveralls, and we are all looking, praying, pleading for work.

Behind the counters, in front of the many lines, are the people who have jobs. On the floor at the beginnings of the lines is tape. The rules are clear. You don't step over this tape until you get the signal from the worker behind the counter. It is amazing to see the different signals used to call people forward. Once the person at the counter who is being helped walks away, the next person in line looks up hopefully. If you are fortunate, you get the immediate head nod. Those who are more cautious will wait for the second head nod to confirm they actually saw the first head nod.

Typically, what happens is that the last person walks away, and the worker behind the counter avoids all eye contact with the next person in line. The worker will shuffle papers, restack papers, organize paper clips, refile and unfile folders, and concentrate on selling the idea that he or she is busier than the president of the

United States. I can't figure out how telling person after person you have no work for them can generate this much paperwork.

All compassion and empathy have long since drained from the faces of the workers. They don't like their jobs, and it is evident by the way they do their jobs. I find some sad humor in this because, given the chance, a room full of people would exchange positions with those on the other side of the sacred counter. We would jump at the opportunity to lose all compassion and empathy for those without jobs.

I initially rest my head against the back wall and then unconsciously begin slowly hitting my head against it. This room is closing in on me and extracting my hope. I follow protocol and wait for my name to be called. I go up to find out there are no positions for me. They tell me to come back in a few weeks to see if any new positions are available. I leave the office and resolve I can never go back.

Slowly, I am coming to the realization that Detroit is not what I hoped it would be for me. On the way back to Shaftsbury, I reflect back on the Detroit I loved so much. On Shaftsbury over the past fourteen years, reality has slowly crept in and taken up residence.

I remember when a woman I used to deliver the paper to was murdered, just two blocks from my house, while I was in grade school. She went to have work done on her car at a local garage. They were going to have to keep the car overnight, so one of the mechanics offered to drive her home. When the mechanic dropped her off, he followed her into the house and killed her. Her son found his mother in the kitchen when he came home from school that day.

There was the cop who moved into Peter's house who *accidently* shot his girlfriend in the pelvis while cleaning his gun. She lived, the relationship didn't, and he was never charged.

In that same house, after the cop moved away, a single father and his two teenage daughters moved in while I was in high school. I became friends with the younger sister and spent hours talking and joking with her. The older sister had a baby with her boyfriend shortly before I left for college. While I was away at college, the boyfriend stormed into the house and shot and killed his girlfriend in the upstairs hallway, and also shot my friend before he exited the house. Fortunately the baby was not harmed. My friend survived and took on the responsibility of raising her nephew as his father was sent to prison.

The quiet street I grew to love is getting louder and louder. The city I so keenly defended to the sheltered whites in college is getting harder and harder to endorse. The city that I fit so well in no longer fits what I want out of life.

On the ride back to Shaftsbury after my MESC experience, I make a decision. I will at least look into Mom's advice and call the headhunter in Toledo, Ohio, a much smaller, calmer city sixty miles south of Detroit. Mom has been trying subtly to get me out of Detroit because her parental vision sees what I have refused to see.

I call the headhunter and meet with her in her small second-floor office in downtown Toledo. She is patient and calm and committed to finding me a job. After a few trips back and forth from Detroit to Toledo, she finds me a great lead on a job with an insurance company, as a claims adjuster. The starting salary is $23,000. Up to this point, the best salary rate I ever made was $10,000 a year. I have no idea what a claims adjuster does, but I am certain I will be a good one.

I fill out the application and remember that, since I can't put my race on the application and my last name is misleading, I had to somehow identify myself as a minority. On my résumé under "Interests," I simply put, "Member of the NAACP." I am desperate, and if my color can help me, I am sure going to use it. I figure it is about time my color is an advantage.

The interview goes very well. So does the second interview. Then I have to sit and wait. At my temp jobs in Detroit, I am praying I will return home to find a message from the insurance company. Finally, the phone rings, and I am moving to Toledo.

Leaving Detroit is sweet with a bitter aftertaste. This city has given me such pride and has helped raise me. The history of the city has had an amazing effect on who I am, and now I leave it to find something better, knowing I will have to live as a minority again. I grieve the loss of comfort, but I am hopeful and excited about finding a better balance. I am confident that after my college experience, I can function in any environment. Maybe Toledo will have something I couldn't find in Detroit.

20

FINALLY ANSWERED

Bending over in front of me behind the counter of Fifth Third Bank is a very cute bank teller. The bank is a mile from my new apartment, and I have found an excuse to come in almost every day. The bank shares space inside the Kroger grocery store at Spring Meadows mall in Toledo, Ohio. I come in frequently, and I take out five to ten dollars. Once this is spent, I return and do it again.

Since I'm new to the area, finding young women my age to talk to me is not easy. I am guaranteed when I come in that she will speak to me if she is free. She has to talk to me; this is her job. I notice her amazing full lips and deep dimples the first time I come to the bank. The dimples and lips are as if God himself drew them on her.

She is friendly, and I can't tell if it is because she has to be or because she wants to be. Her nametag reads "Shilease."

My skills with women need a lot of work. I learned early in life that I may not be the coolest and most dashing fellow, but if I get the chance to speak and can show my charm and sense of humor, that makes up for my un-Denzel-like appearance. The challenge has always been getting up the courage to start the conversation.

I was introduced to my current girlfriend, who lives in Detroit, by a close high school friend, which made things much easier for me. Since my move, I only see her on the weekends, and my weeks are long and lonely. The fact that I am lonely helps justify my desire to talk to the teller in front of me.

Watching this petite young lady behind the counter sends a surge of courage through my veins. My body has decided before my brain that I am going to have to find a way to ask this young lady out.

Distracted by her tight purple suede miniskirt, I try to complete my deposit slip, but my eyes keep drifting to see more purple suede. She turns around, and quickly I divert my eyes to my paperwork, hoping she did not see me looking at her nice curvy miniskirt.

Her smile is electric, and my courage surges again. I cannot speak because the pounding of my heart in my ears is deafening. She takes my deposit, I thank her, and I walk away, dazed. My transactions over the past few months have only involved seeing her from her tiny waist up. This is the first time I have seen more of her. It is such a shock to me I totally forget to withdrawal any money. The embarrassment of returning today is too much for my system to handle. I will come back tomorrow.

Since high school, I have dated pretty regularly. After the experiences I had in college with dating, I concluded that the added hassle involved with dating someone from another race just wasn't worth it. It is not something I am against for others, but my shoulders are not broad enough to bear that cross.

There is one other reason why I have gravitated to black girls. Ever since I noticed girls in school, the emphasis was always on their shapely figures. Besides color, this is the biggest difference in cultures that I have experienced. The black community celebrates the women with the more curvy figures. If you are a black girl with no hips, you lose the attention to the black girl with hips. This is the polar opposite of the white culture. If you are white and have too many curves, you are considered fat and generally less desirable.

Growing up, the only girls I came in contact with on a regular basis were the black girls in school. I grew up being attracted to more shapely black girls.

My teller at the bank is black and very attractive, and having seen her bend over, I realize she fills the last requirement as well. Now how am I going to harness the courage to ask her out?

I have not found an answer to that question before I return the next day to withdraw money so I can eat.

I'm waiting in line and see her perfect smile and beautiful lips as she speaks politely to customers ahead of me. I think she looks up and smiles at me, but I am unsure. I am standing in line doing Lamaze techniques to try and slow down my heart, so I can hear and speak. I start counting off customers to see if she will wait on me.

"OK, if this guy in front of me is quick, and the customer at the other window takes a little longer, I should get Shilease," I think to myself.

God smiles on me, and it goes as planned. The customer in front of me makes a quick deposit and is gone. I step to the window, and before I can push something out that I pray is English, she speaks.

"You're lucky I am your teller."

I think to myself, "I know. Thank you, Jesus!" but I say nothing. I smile and she continues.

"I checked your deposit, and you wrote the wrong account number on your deposit slip yesterday. Don't worry—I changed it," she says.

I say to myself, "I love how your dimples and lips move when you talk."

I graciously thank her and withdraw my usual five dollars. As she is processing my request, we make small talk, and I swear she is flirting with me, but I'm not certain. I thank her again for correcting my mistake, and I leave trying to think of what I will say when I return tomorrow for another five dollars.

On my way home, something occurs to me. I remember, from being a teller on my summer breaks during college, that there is no reason for a teller to check someone's deposit slip. When you take in a deposit, you attach the deposit slip to the check and put it in your outbox. Later, the check and deposit slip get sent down to the proof department. The errors are caught in the proof department, *not* at the teller window. So why was she studying my deposit slip so closely?

Remembering back to my teller days, I recall my process if a cute girl came into the bank. I would hold her paperwork to the side, and when I got a chance later, I would use the paperwork to look up her information. There I could find out if she was married, who else was on the account, and how old she was.

Is this what Shilease is doing? Is she checking me out?

She *was* flirting with me!

I only need a little encouragement to act. I am tired of playing "what if." Passing my apartment, I head straight for the florist. I send a bouquet of flowers directly to the bank, addressed to Shilease. I attach a card that reads, "Thanks for correcting my mistakes. Call me. Kevin Hofmann." Then I write my number. Again my heart is racing, and testosterone is doing laps in my veins. I am in such a hurry to do this because I fear the courage will retreat.

Returning home, I juggle back and forth in my mind whether I should have sent the flowers or not. The relief of finally doing something is attacked by the preoccupation that I may have read the situation wrong. I conclude that this will force an answer, good or bad, by tomorrow.

After I finish dinner and watch some TV in my small apartment, I decide to go to bed early. Sleep will make tomorrow come sooner. Before I go to bed, I call my girlfriend in Detroit. The conversation is cut short because I can't concentrate on two women at once. "The long day has worn me out," is my excuse, and I cut the nightly talk short and go to bed. The guilt I harbor in my chest also makes it uncomfortable to talk to the unsuspecting girl in Detroit.

My eight-hour workday seems like a week. Finally, I am dismissed, and I hurry home to check my answering machine. The machine is empty. I check all cords and make sure there is nothing wrong with the phone mechanically. I check to make sure there is a tape in the machine also. There is a tape in the machine.

She has not called.

Tomorrow, I will have to find another bank. What I thought was a straight fastball was a curve. I swung for the rooftop and hit nothing but air. My pride is damaged, and I comfort myself that I still have a girlfriend in Detroit.

As I am fixing my usual entrée for dinner, cream-style corn, and dancing to the music from my portable stereo (I am a great dancer alone in my apartment), I reassure myself that Shilease let one get away. My confidence is just about back to full when the phone rings.

I freeze.

The corn is bubbling in the pot, the music is loud, and the phone is on the second ring. I have to turn down the stove, turn off the music, and get to the phone in the living room in two rings before the machine picks up. For the first time, I am thankful my apartment is so small. In one leap, the stove and radio are off, and I am diving to the phone.

"Hello?" Calm is how I hope I sound, but desperate and out of breath is probably more accurate.

"Hi, this is Shilease from the bank. Thank you for my flowers."

She sounds great on the phone!

"Thanks for taking care of those mistakes for me," I say, able to regain some composure.

"You put the wrong phone number on the card. I had to look up your correct number."

She cares enough to look up the right number. *Yes!*

The conversation flows easily and smoothly. After about ten minutes of good conversation, my self-esteem has been restored, and I can tell I read the situation right.

Confidently, I say, "So where are we going to go tomorrow after you get off work?" I hold my breath, hoping that came out as smooth as I thought it would.

She answers without a pause. "I don't know. Where do you want to go?"

She sounds great on the phone!

"How about the movies? We can go see *Harlem Nights* with Eddie Murphy."

"That would be fine," she says.

Touchdown! Home run! Extra point! Field goal!

We begin to see each other regularly. I spend as much time as I can with her. Her easy personality is great. She is smart, kind, and quick to put me in check. I like that.

Weeks dissolve into months, and we continue to see each other Monday through Thursday. On Friday, I pack up and go to Detroit to see my girlfriend and friends back in Detroit. I like the attention I get through dating and always have. There is something about dating that fills me up inside. To date two women at the same time is hectic, and the guilt that I feel nags at me. I try to push it away, but when I am alone, the guilt sneaks up on me. The attention feeds my ego, and being wanted by two women fills a hole in me and artificially inflates my self-esteem. For now the need to be liked outweighs the guilt.

Shilease and I meet in May of 1990, and by August of that same year the guilt of running back and forth begins to tip the scales. I come clean and tell Shilease about the girl in Detroit.

Casually, she says, "I know." She is hurt, but her confident ways tell her not to show it.

We continue Monday through Thursday, and I think since nothing more is said, it is OK. My ego convinces me to only respond when Shilease calls. I stop calling her, and my cool, nonchalant attitude when she does call is rude at best.

Suddenly, the messages that used to be there when I come home from Detroit aren't there. Shilease stops calling. She cuts me off, no explanation, and disappears. The relationship I thought I had total control over is unraveling. After several weeks of being without this light in my life, I put my ego in the hallway and call Shilease.

"Hey, how are you? Are your fingers broken? How come you don't call me anymore?" I calmly say.

I don't hear what she says back. The fact that she is still talking to me is a great relief. The message is clear. She won't take my crap. I like that.

It is now late fall, and although my trips to Detroit are still happening, they are happening less and less. The need to fill this deficiency in me is still there, and I am unwilling to cut off one of the sources feeding me. Shilease and I spend all our free time together, and I enjoy her company.

As Christmas comes and goes, someone speaks to me. In a rare instance when I am alone in my apartment, I hear a voice say, "She is so nice to you. Why do you treat her so cruelly?"

Although I have been nicer to her than I was a few months ago, I am still seeing the girl in Detroit. I am aware Shilease has feelings for me, but I am still seeing the girl in Detroit. In an instant, I know the answer and what I must do.

I make a final trip to Detroit and end the relationship. I finally act on a decision I should have made several months ago.

When I return to Toledo, I go over to Shilease's house, explain I have ended the relationship in Detroit, and beg her to forgive me. We decide to start things fresh, and I thank God for her.

We are now inseparable. I pick her up from work and bring her to my apartment. We see each other Sunday through Saturday. The only time we don't see each other is when we are working.

I introduce her to the Detroit family and to Mom and Dad, and she is brought into both families.

We date for another six months, and we talk about getting married. At this point, we have been together for over a year. We decide we are ready, and we will get engaged soon. I just don't tell her when or where.

By now Shilease has a key to my apartment. I tell her I am going out after work and ask her to stop by after she gets off work. She knows she will be there before me.

While she is at work, I buy two dozen silk white roses. I make a path from the front door to the dining-room table. On the table is the ring box. Shilease comes in and follows the rose path to the dining-room table. As she gets to the table and sees the ring box, I step out of the bedroom dressed in my best suit.

"You didn't think I would be here to ask you this, did you? Will you marry me?" I softly ask.

"Yes," she softly says back. She sounds good.

We arrange to get married in sixteen months. We take the time to plan and organize and arrange and get to know each other.

In September of 1993, we get married. The left side of the church is her friends and family, mostly black. On the right side of the church are my friends and family, mostly white. Mike and Joe are beside me when Shilease and I get married.

Over the next two years we struggle, both financially and as a young married couple. We somehow get a bank to loan us money, and we buy a house in a black neighborhood soon after Shilease is pregnant. She gets bigger and more beautiful with each day, and she puts up with an immature husband who never knows the right thing to say or do.

In 1996 we have our first son, Tai Malik.

Finally, there is someone in my family who has part of me in him.

He is a well-behaved baby. He is thoughtful and investigates everything with his eyes. He makes parenting an ease and a joy.

I later find out a blood relative is a present Shilease was anxious to give me. It is a powerful moment for me in ways that most take for granted. Our son is light skinned like me and a piece of my incomplete puzzle.

Four years later his brother, Zion Mekhi, is born. He is the polar opposite of his quiet brother. Our new son investigates with his hands. This often leads to a mess or something broken. He teaches me patience. He has Shilease's skin tone and her perfect round head.

Again I share DNA with someone I know. When I sit and feed my sons or pick them up, I wonder what their biological grandmother would say. She can't help but love them. They are adorable.

I envision the day I will introduce them to her. She still runs through my thoughts, and every now and then I dance with the fantasy of her. Seeing my own sons, I realize this meeting will have to be attempted. I have a desire for her to see my boys. She would be so proud.

The idea of her being proud is a new idea, but deep under my heart is a need for her to be proud of me. I want her to be relieved that the choice she made was a good one and that I turned out all right. The search for her is not over. The seed of desire is planted again, and this time it has a few extra branches. The particulars of when I will search for her again are not yet pressing.

My move to Toledo fills many holes and creates a scenario for even more to be filled.

21

JOURNEY TO 1600 PENNSYLVANIA

As I lie on our black leather couch in the living room, tears from my right eye race the tears from my left eye down my cheeks. CNN has just announced that Senator Obama is the projected winner of Ohio in the 2008 presidential election. This declaration assures him the historical victory.

I am wrestling with the emotions that have built up in my chest as they seek a way to escape; the emotions seep out through my tears. I struggle to hold back the sobs welling up in me. In the middle of this internal altercation, my eight-year-old, Zion, walks into the room. Upon hearing that Senator Obama has won Ohio, he walks over to me without saying a word. He bends down and he hugs me. His tight, exaggerated hug conveys understanding that he couldn't possibly know. I hug him back, thankful he is able to witness this at such a young age. I hold him close until the fountain in my eyes shuts off. We disconnect, and my son retreats back to the den to watch Cartoon Network without saying a word.

It is officially announced that Senator Obama is now President-Elect Obama. He appears on stage in Chicago at Grant Park to give his acceptance speech with Michelle, Sasha, and Malia, and never have I seen such a powerful picture. The Obamas are the Huxtables times a thousand. President-Elect Obama gives his acceptance speech in the eloquent way we have come to expect, and my cheeks are soaked again.

This time, Tai, my twelve-year-old, comes over to me. He too bends down and hugs me. As he hugs me, he simply says,

"Let it out, Dad." He somehow knows I am trying to keep my composure, trying to push down the emotion that is once again erupting in my chest. It takes all the strength I have to avoid the Jesse Jackson ugly cry. But in the end it is useless. The tears gush as I hug my oldest son back.

While I am a wet mess on the couch, Shilease is on the laptop looking for a hotel room for the inauguration. She secures the closest one we can find, in Baltimore, Maryland, and on January 20, 2009, we will be in DC to witness President Obama being sworn in at the Capitol Building.

It is January 19, 2009, around 10:00 p.m., and the four of us make it to our room in a Baltimore hotel. Shilease checks all the information, and we decide to get up in four hours to start our journey into DC.

At 2:00 a.m. we are up getting dressed and quickly walking out the door. We make it to the Green Belt train station by 3:30 a.m., just when the parking lot is supposed to open. The parking lot is full.

We continue on to the next station at College Park; we get right into the garage and catch the first train to DC. We exit the train station at the Federal Center, and the station is packed with people. It is a claustrophobic's night terror. I feel pressure from the crowd that surrounds me from every side. We and the crowd gel into one large mass as we make our way up the stairs and out to the street. I grab my youngest son's hand, Shilease grabs our oldest son's hand and my back pocket, and we flow with the crowd. Once we break free of the station, it is instant relief, and the crowd disperses into the city.

It is still nighttime dark out, but the lights of the city are beautiful. We fall in line with the group and head toward the mall in front of the Capitol Building. After some confusion, and an occasional area where people are close enough that we exchange DNA, we arrive on the mall at about 5:30 a.m. We camp out in the crowd in front of a large TV monitor, about a quarter mile away from the Capitol Building. Once we stop moving, the cooler-than-normal January air attacks us.

All week the forecast was for temperatures in the thirties. Instead we get temperatures in the teens with a wind. As we stand on the mall in the large, open field, the wind cuts us like a razor-sharp knife.

We are surrounded by people, and the scene is unlike anything I have ever seen.

The most popular guy in the crowd is the guy giving out small American flags. People rush to him like he is handing out money. The second-most-popular guy is the businessman who thought ahead. He has boxes and boxes of hand-warming packets for sale. I am sure, with just those around us, we pay for his child's college education.

To the right of us is a large group sitting on the ground wrapped in blankets. Behind us is a tall, heavy-set white man who appears to be alone. He hands his nice, new, expensive video camera to a black teenaged girl. She is a stranger before she holds the camera. He asks her to just film whatever she can until the battery runs out. He wants her to capture this day for him. In front of us, an Asian woman in her twenties has an autograph book that she is passing around to anyone who will sign it.

As we stand there, trying to forget the cold, someone begins singing, "We Shall Overcome," and the crowd joins in. The singing continues throughout the morning sporadically, mostly gospel songs. After about an hour, our youngest son decides to sit on the ground. He sits with his legs crossed, head down, hood up, and hands in his coat. He falls asleep on the cold mall gravel. Our oldest son decides to stand huddled close to Shilease and me.

People continue to pour into the mall and walk through the crowd. We are packed so tightly that as they walk by they do not realize our eight-year-old is huddled on the ground. I station myself around him to prevent him from being stepped on. Shilease does the same, and we cover him. A woman behind us takes up the job of traffic cop. She directs everyone who passes around our son who is camped out on the ground.

At about 8:00 a.m., after the sun has risen over the Capitol Building, Shilease decides we have to move around, and I agree. By this point, I can feel my bone marrow freezing. I bend down to wake our little camper, and at first he doesn't move. Immediately,

I fear he has passed out because of the cold. After two or three shakes, he rises, and we begin to walk around. We walk toward the Capitol Building and realize there still is plenty of room up ahead. Unfortunately, our eight-year-old is now shivering uncontrollably. Shilease and I decide we have to get him back to the hotel. We make our way off the mall, and soon we are in the middle of another mob. It appears several hundred people decide the cold wins at about the same time. This crowd is packed closer than any crowd we have faced yet. We don't move unless the mob says so, and when the mob moves, we obey. Suddenly, a large white man comes up behind Shilease and asks if she is trying to leave. Shilease replies, "I am just trying not to lose my children."

"OK," he replies. "That guy in the red is about to open up a hole. Follow him."

The guy in the red instantly parts the crowd better than Moses parted the Red Sea. We shoot through the hole and are instantly off the mall, and the cool air feels good in my lungs.

Our plan is to walk back to the train station and catch the train back to Baltimore.

After walking all over DC for the next ninety minutes looking for a train station that has trains leaving the city, we find out that all the trains exiting the city are shut down until further notice. We are now trapped out in the cold.

Our youngest son, who is normally a talker, hasn't said anything in the last ninety minutes. I look behind me, and our oldest is now limping because his new boots are cutting into his right heel. Shilease, who is usually the toughest of all of us, looks cold, miserable, and worried about her boys. I am helpless and wonder why I even attempted this crazy outing.

As my protective-husband-and-father mind searches for a solution, I remember seeing a coach bus a few blocks back that had a small sign in the front window that read, "Warming bus." We make our way to Twelfth Street and Pennsylvania and back to the bus. The driver opens the door and gladly welcomes us. The bus is running and warm. We take our seats, shed hats and gloves, and let the warm air hit our cold skin.

The chairs are soft and comfortable and such a welcomed luxury. It is now about 10:00 a.m., and the driver puts in an old movie, and we watch it on the many monitors on the bus. We all take a nap in the warmth.

At 11:00 a.m. the bus driver turns off the movie and turns on the radio. We hear a play-by-play of where President-Elect Obama is until he makes it to the Capitol, and the ceremony begins. I sit in my seat with my head pressed against the cold glass of the window, and I listen to what I thought was impossible.

My ears are flooded with the words of Pastor Rick Warren as he gives the opening prayer. My tears begin to flow as I think about my forty-one years of life—a life that began with a cross burned on the lawn of my first home.

Aretha Franklin fills the bus with her beautiful voice, a voice I have heard so often growing up in Detroit, but today she sounds more pure than I ever remember. I reflect on my life to this point, to this day, and I am overwhelmed. The constant battle between black and white in me and around me all vanishes. My heart leaps as Vice President Biden is sworn in, and my heart beats with joy as President Obama says the sacred oath.

Several times earlier in the day, I thought this trip was a huge mistake. Initially, I am heartbroken because we aren't on the mall when President Obama recites the oath. I realize that where we are, we are meant to be. We are on a quiet bus, warm and comfortable, away from the distractions of a large crowd, away from the distractions like Aretha's hat, which would steal attention away from this powerful moment in history. My good friend Joe Tenbusch later will point out the significance of being on a bus at this time, and my heart understands this is no mistake.

As we ride back to the hotel on the train, the scene on the mall becomes much clearer. In the crowds so thick and so close the person next to me could hear my thoughts, I never heard one angry word. As the crowd pushed and it felt like I was going to implode from the pressure, no one ever got upset, no one yelled, and my family and I were in a vacuum with two million other people.

On this amazing day, not one person is arrested. I need to say that again because my mind can't comprehend that thought. Over two million people are gathered, and not *one* person is arrested.

I can almost assure you that at every sporting event I have ever gone to in my life with more than five thousand people, someone was arrested.

The next day we return to DC to take the kids around to the different sites. Our first stop is the White House. Shilease and I have been there before, but this Wednesday in 2009 is special. We take pictures of the boys in front of the White House, and I imagine what President Obama and his family are doing in this beautiful home. I picture how nice it would be to be inside the White House, and I simply think to myself, "I will just wait until one of the boys gets elected."

This thought stops me—cold—and it has nothing to do with the temperature. I have never entertained that thought for myself. This impossible day never even penetrated my fantasies. It was too far out to even pretend for me. The ceiling that I grew up under is gone, and my sons' futures are limitless. *Limitless!*

My black-and-white world is not the world my sons now live in. The struggle that Mom and Dad faced behind the scenes while I grew up will not be our boys' struggle. As a father, I am relieved that the ugly that walked side by side with us will not stalk my boys.

Racism is not erased. The heart of prejudice is still beating, but the change I've seen in forty-two years is heart stopping.

We now live in a diverse neighborhood. The black neighborhood that the boys were born in became too much. Over the thirteen years Shilease and I lived in that neighborhood, gradually, just as I saw Detroit ooze into Shaftsbury Street as I was growing up, I saw hope exit the black neighborhood in Toledo.

As hope exited, despair replaced it, and the "I will get you before you get me" mentality that I remember from Whitcomb Street flowed down our street. Shilease and I made the decision to move to this more diverse neighborhood that leaves room for hope.

As the boys run out to play with their black, white, and Asian friends, I catch my tongue and hold it. The father in me wants to warn them of the dangers and prejudice that may be beyond our front door. I want to warn them of the pitfalls I experienced when I grew up. It takes all the strength in me to be silent. The realization that their time is different tells me to shut up.

"Their experience is not your experience. Don't taint them with your fears," wisdom tells me as they head out the door for the park. Greater wisdom tells me that someday, I will have to explain the truth and possibility of how race can affect them: to ignore that would be more tragic than tainting their safe world.

It doesn't matter if you agree with the selection of the forty-fourth president or not. The fact that the majority of Americans said yes to a black president has changed our world in ways I can't imagine. If you are American, that has to make you proud. It makes me proud to be a part of this time in history, and thinking about what that means for my boys makes my cheeks moist again.

The extraordinary changes in America that have taken place throughout my life cause me to reflect on the extraordinary results I have seen because of an extraordinary decision Mom and Dad made forty-two years ago.

22

EXTRAORDINARY RESULTS

Grandma was right.

What Mom and Dad did was out of the ordinary. The decision they made to put "biracial" on their list for potential adoptees, which eventually led them to my adoption, was extraordinary—not in a heroic sort of way but in an "out of the ordinary" way. Because this was such an out-of-the-box, off-the-wall idea, it changed the way they would look at things, and that meant they would have to make some extraordinary decisions. Some of those decisions were agonizing, I'm sure.

The decision to move to a black neighborhood to assure their new black child had a firm foundation was groundbreaking. The thought that it had to be done even at the expense of their white children was, I am sure, something they lost sleep over. The decision after five years of living in the black neighborhood to leave and move to a white neighborhood at the expense of their one black child but to preserve the family again stole many more nights of sleep. These decisions were extreme but necessary, extraordinary but vital, and they were all rooted in the first decision that pushed this ball in motion. Many similar life-changing decisions would come and go, and after recounting this history, I sit and wonder if it was all worth it. Was the cost of this one decision too expensive? Did the risks outweigh the gains?

A good friend of mine recently said to me, "You came out pretty normal, growing up the way you did." On the surface, he was right. I came out closer to normal than you would expect. But his comment caused me to dig deep, to really challenge myself, and to see if my surface matched my core. I was intrigued by the idea of diving into my own history and examining the effects of a transracial adoption and the life of a transracial adoptee. I began to examine just how I was affected by this unusual life and what results flowed from it. In this examination, I hoped to find out if the price paid was too high.

I HAVE ISSUES

Driving down a dark highway four years ago, I was listening to talk radio. The professional was talking about adoption. His theory was that a large majority of kids who have been adopted struggle with feelings of rejection and issues with self-esteem. After about two minutes of listening to his theory, I concluded he had no idea what he was talking about and began surfing the radio for something that would keep my attention.

Over the next several weeks, this theory kept coming back to me. After dismissing it as psychobabble the first five or six times, I decided to entertain the thought that he may know a little of what he was talking about. The more I thought about it, the more sense it made. In my own little quiet space, I had to admit, I have issues.

My self-talk changed from "There is no truth in this theory" into "There could be some sense in what he says." I began to surrender to the idea that a child may feel rejected after being given up for adoption.

The most powerful bond in nature is said to be between mother and child, and if you are a child who was given up by your mother and placed for adoption, it is understandable that you could have some feelings of rejection.

My next thought process went to a more personal level. I had to wrestle with the idea that *I* may have those issues. To this point, I liked the idea that I was basically unaffected by the adoption process and had come through this crazy experience with no issues or scars.

This one statement by some unknown quack caused me to question if I was truly normal. I was in my thirties, and I was finally at the age where I chose to look beyond the surface. How deep I would scratch below the surface was not known at this time, but I was open to doing a little probing

Part of me felt bad about giving in to this thought. I was so blessed that I had landed with the family I had. I was so blessed to be adopted into a family who cared so strongly for me, a family who made so many unbelievable sacrifices for me. It felt like I was cheating on them by entertaining some of these feelings that I had buried for so long.

One conclusion I came up with was that the two were separate. The adoption was an amazing experience for me and a great success story. My family was great and loved me like no one else could. Period.

The deeper issues I may have had were all right to feel. No matter how or why my mother gave me away, it happened, and I had to deal with that fact. I did have some feelings of rejection. On the surface, I understood it was a very selfless act to give me up so I could have a better life than she thought she could give me. I understood it. I understood it. I understood it.

This understanding did not make the nagging go away. Over the next several months, I came to accept that I did have these feelings and that this was all right. These feelings of rejection were identified and singular. They did not come with bitterness or anger. As I said, I understood the reasons behind the choice to give me up for adoption. My brain got it.

My heart mourned the loss of my biological mother and was stuck on being given away. The reasoning was simple—since my birth mother did not keep me and no one stole me from her, she gave me away.

When my heart spoke that truth to my brain, my brain understood the theory that from this came feelings of rejection. How could you avoid those feelings?

How this feeling of rejection affected my life was my next puzzle. Did it really affect me? After turning it over and over in my mind, I faced some startling thoughts.

What came to mind were several examples of how I have stopped short of my potential. I recalled the time in college when I was running track my freshman year. At a track meet during a race, instead of turning as the track turned, I ran straight off the track and quit. On the surface it was simple. I was tired of running, so I just stopped. There was more to it. Through the years, I had become a master of justification. I told myself it was because this team was horrible. My high school track team could have beaten my college team easily. This was probably true, but the deeper reason I quit was because I was afraid of succeeding.

The potential to be better than I had ever imagined was there. Deep down I knew if I committed to really working at it, I would be good, very good. That chance at being great scared me. So I did the easy thing: I pushed the buttons to activate the imploding sequence.

At the state meet in high school, I did the same thing. I was less than twelve hours away from living up to my potential. My routine was simple, and I did everything against it. Prior to this race, everything I did was in preparation of the next race. The night before this big, important race, I handed it away. Again the sequence was activated.

My professional working career followed the same pattern. I moved up quickly in my first job. All that I did was done to move up the corporate ladder. Just as I was about to really explode, the rebel in me purposely said the wrong thing to the wrong person, and almost instantly my skyrocketing career was shut down.

The feeling of rejection manifested itself over and over again. My mind told me I was not good enough, so whenever greatness was possible, I quit. I found a way to step out before I found out if I could be great or not. Being my own enemy, there was no way to win.

This has continued as I have tried several businesses that never made it. Shilease and I started a stationery business that had potential to make us, at the minimum, some good side money. Before it took off, as I saw the potential, I stopped working at it and let it dissolve.

Years later I discovered a hidden talent in working with wood. I began making these beautiful pieces of art. The work I did had potential to make a lot of money if marketed to the right people. The chance at success scared me off again. I put down the tools and justified it by saying no one would pay me what the pieces were worth—again, another external excuse for my internal problem.

Then I developed the skill to make pens out of wood. Again this was a God-given talent that just appeared out of thin air. There was a demand for the pens, and their uniqueness made them valuable. Just as this new business was taking off, so did I. I put the tools down again and walked away.

While dating, this low self-esteem and feelings of rejection are why I felt the need to date several people at once. As I stated earlier, the attention I got from dating filled a void. The void's beginnings were rooted in these issues. I was afraid of rejection, so I clung to more than one woman; that way, if one rejected me, I still had the other. Dating more than one woman at a time also triggers the self-destruction sequence because it was always a matter of time before I was caught.

This book was started and stopped many times until finally I was sick and tired of being average. Underneath my issues I have always felt a calling to be great, a calling to be bigger than myself. That drive on the dark highway changed my life. The realization that I was my worst enemy in so many situations was frustrating and empowering. When you are the problem, you are also the solution.

If you are reading this book that you purchased in a bookstore or online, it is a testament that I conquered my fear of success. This is a great example of pushing past the voices that have always said, "You are not good enough. You do not deserve to be more than average." This project screams over the voices that I have given so much life to over the years.

Now that I know the root cause of my actions, I can change how I respond to things.

The inclination to drift in the direction that is less than me is still there. The fear of rejection causes me to shy away from relationships. The natural urge to go off by myself when in a crowded room or to stay quiet instead of start up a conversation with someone still sits on my shoulder. This urge may never retreat, but now that I know it is there, I can push through it and force myself to act in a way that is more productive. Gaining the knowledge of my issues and their origin has been an empowering experience.

IN MY OWN SKIN

Toward the end of high school and through college, I went through my "black phase." There was a fear that my blackness would be rubbed off because I lived in an all-white home environment. To combat that, I became black. My favorite T-shirt was one I bought at the African festival in Detroit. It was black and had the outline of Africa on the front. On the back it said, "It's a black thing—you wouldn't understand." I would wear around my neck a leather medallion in the shape of Africa.

At about this time, I also was a part of a rap group called General Principle. It was a group made up of friends from high school.

Derrick Louis was the leader, and we would sit and write lyrics to raps song. The raps were very pro-black and anti–white establishment. We often sat at the Hofmann dining-room table and shared the raps we wrote. Mom would often be within earshot, and she would no doubt hear our venom.

My rap career was cut short when the other members of the group thought I sounded too proper. I was ruining the group's street credibility, so I was axed. Derrick, who had become a very close friend, sat me down and advised that my services were no longer needed. Part of me was hurt because I still could not shake the anchor of talking proper. A larger part of me was relieved. The lyrics of our raps made me uneasy, and I agreed that I did lack the tough edge that the others in the group possessed.

There is no way, as I look back now, that I couldn't have offended Mom and Dad with my new "enlightened" path. They rode out this phase with me, allowing me to express myself in a not-so-productive way.

I created the fear that one color will drown out the other or water it down. My fear was that the result would be a shade in between the two, leaving me stuck in the middle, not being comfortable or accepted in either side.

The majority of the blacks on campus did not want me around, and the whites did not want me around either. Being caught in the gap between the two was a real fear.

Later, I learned this was more a result of me not being friendly. The wall I put up worked well to keep people out, both white and black.

There are environments where I still feel uncomfortable. Being in an all-white environment still makes me uneasy. The game of trying to figure out if a gesture or comment is racially motivated or the result of the person just not liking me is still a game I struggle at.

There are some black environments that I find uncomfortable. There are situations where some blacks don't think I am black enough. When I was younger this would bother me because I hated being rejected because of something I had no control over. In recent years, it stopped bothering me. There is no way I will convince them otherwise, and it isn't worth my time and energy.

The issues that I have and my maturation with myself are not just my issues. I realize many people who weren't adopted struggle with these same issues. My reflection on my life has pointed out to me that these are issues that have come from growing up as I did as an adoptee, but I am not hoarding these issues as my own, and they are not issues solely related to adoptees. I am also not blaming my adoption for my issues. I am simply stating that these are things I have struggled with, and this is where I think they are rooted. The fact that other people who weren't adopted struggle with these issues supports that I am not alone. This also supports the idea that I am more normal than not. If I didn't have issues, one could argue, that would make me more abnormal.

EXTRAORDINARY RESULTS

From the one extraordinary decision and the many extraordinary choices came some extraordinary results. If I were given the chance to start over in life, I would choose to change...*nothing*. The love that I have received from my parents is overwhelming. I often ask myself, as a father, "Could I have made those sacrifices? Could I have endured what Mom and Dad did for my boys?" Honestly, I just don't know.

The life that my sister Lisa and brothers James and Matthew endured was not easy. They were forced to live as minorities in several situations, and for my brothers, especially, I know that was not always a setting they welcomed. I feel some responsibility for the struggles they were forced to endure because of me and have recently come to realize my brothers and I are not as close as I would like because of the life we lived. Their sacrifices may just have been too great.

Fortunately, Lisa enjoyed the experiences. She recently told me she appreciated living life as a minority. She explained that living as a minority really taught her what life is like for other people. For my sister, this was a positive and life-changing experience, an experience she says she was fortunate to walk through. Regardless of how it was seen when we were going through it, its effects on our family and those around us are powerful.

To appreciate the extraordinary result, you need only look at the marriages and choices made by my family and the families around us.

My sister Lisa was the first to get married. She married a black man she met while in the air force. They have a beautiful biracial daughter.

James married a woman from China, and they have a daughter as well.

Matthew married a woman from China also. They have a son. Their marriage didn't last, and Matthew remarried. In his second marriage, Matthew married a woman from Japan. They have a son and a daughter.

The colors of our family are obvious and a testament to the beautiful lessons we learned growing up. Whether my siblings agreed with our upbringing or not, you can't help but see the effects our life had on their adult lives.

The marriage of color has extended to my close friends from Shaftsbury.

My best friend, Mike, married a woman from Puerto Rico, and they have two girls and one boy. Mike cofounded a nonprofit agency in inner-city Detroit that helps thousands of children every year.

Mike's younger brother, Joe, majored in African Studies at the University of Michigan and still knows more about my culture than I do. He married a woman from Hungary, and they later divorced. He is now a principal at a black high school in Chicago. He too lives a life rich with color.

Jose Galano, the boy I flipped off the first week I moved to Shaftsbury Street, grew up and married a woman from the Detroit area, who is white, and they adopted two children from Guatemala. I tear up when I think of the evolution of Jose that I had the privilege of witnessing. Jose is the friend and brother I am most proud of.

The tree that was planted when my Mom and Dad adopted me grew and spawned branch after branch that went in so many directions. I laugh today when I look at my immediate family.

Besides Mom and Dad, I am the only one who married in the same race.

Three years ago, Grandma died. The last days of her life, she was a very difficult person to be around. She was always very judgmental of everyone throughout her life. Now her increasing age gave her the excuse to say anything to anybody. She made life at the nursing home hell for my mother, who cared for her daily, and for the nursing-home staff.

In the last three years of her life, whenever I saw her, she would make sure to comment on how much weight I had gained (another form of my sabotage). I had grown accustomed to her criticism and chose to deal with it by seeing her less and less.

Grandma's critiques continued every time I saw her in the nursing home. They were not racially motivated. I knew that, but I was just tired of hearing about how fat I was.

The last time I saw Grandma alive, she was lying in her bed at the nursing home. She was in and out of sleep. When she woke up, I was standing at the end of her bed, and she looked at me. She reached for me, and I moved toward her and grabbed her hand. Her hands were like Aunt Theresa's and Aunt Ruth's from years ago, worn and soft and covered with loose skin. Grandma looked me in my face and quietly said, "Oh, Kevin, you look OK."

Where she used to say, "Oh, Kevin, you're still putting on the weight," or something similar, she said I looked "OK."

On the ride home, my wife, Shilease, explained to me the significance of what Grandma had said. I was so conditioned to being called fat, I was just relieved she did not do it again.

Grandma was saying so much more in the only way she knew how. These were the last words Grandma said to me, and I am still trying to come to the same realization.

The changes I saw in friends and family, in my street and community, and within my own chest make it easy to answer the questions that began this chapter. Because of this one extraordinary decision made over forty years ago, I have been fortunate to witness many extraordinary results from an extraordinary life growing up black in white.

23

LESSONS FROM THE LIFE

Over the past seven years I have learned so much about myself and this life as a transracial adoptee, which are shared in the section below. I hope you take the time to read them and incorporate them into your family's journey. They will help you raise amazing wonderful-beyond-measure children.

"Hi, Kev, it's Dad!"

Dad didn't get caller ID, so I acted surprised, as if I hadn't seen his name flash across my iPhone screen. "How are you?"

"I'm good," Dad replied, sounding distracted and anxious to get to his point for calling. "Hey, Kev, I was calling because I was just thinking, and I want you to speak at my funeral. Would you do that for me?" Dad has always been preoccupied with his own death and dying. This combined with his dementia resulted in today's urgency. Today's obsession was his funeral, and I rolled with it.

"Sure, I can do that," I said without a pause.

"Great! I will put together some of the things I would like you to talk about. But I don't want you to tell people how great I was. I don't want to hear that crap!" Dad said, sounding irritated. Dad has always been hard on himself when it comes to his own achievements. I also think, as a pastor, he has been at too many funerals where people have been romanticized and fictionalized.

He wanted to stay true to his calling and make sure the funeral was more about his faith and less about him.

"I can do that, Dad. Just let me know what you would like me to say. I will not tell everyone how great you were," I said flatly.

"Good! I'll put some things together and get it to you. Well, now that that is taken care of, how are the boys and Shilease?" he said, smoothly switching subjects.

"They are good!" I replied.

"Good. Well, I'll let you go. Take care of yourself, and I'll talk to you soon."

"OK, Dad! Talk to you soon," I said as I hit the end button on my phone.

This conversation took place in February of 2015. Quickly the dementia descended upon Dad. It was like God was slowly pulling down the window shade in Dad's life; less and less light was getting in during each conversation. Over the next two months we would speak often, and every now and then the funeral conversation would come up, and I would promise not to tell everyone he was great.

The conversations began to make less sense, and his thought process was harder and harder to follow. He would often go on a rant that seemed like an endless loop where he would restate the same thing almost verbatim several times. He, along with our conversations, faded quickly. By late March, talking on the phone was no longer possible. I would go visit, and he would sleep most of the time. Occasionally, he would wake up and mumble, "Oh, hey, Kev."

"Hi, Dad!" I'd say, being sincerely excited to talk to him this time. "How are you feeling?"

"I'm tired. I just can't shake this flu bug." His mental illness lied to him that he was merely suffering from a cold. "How are Shilease and the boys?"

"They're doing well. They told me to tell you hi."

"Oh, good," Dad would say as his shade inched down farther and he drifted off to sleep.

I stayed a while longer while he slept, and as I got up to leave, Dad rolled over. "Oh, hey, Kev," Dad said again as if we hadn't seen each other in a while.

"Hey, Dad. I got to go. I'll see you tomorrow." I bent over and kissed him on the forehead three times. The three kisses are trademark in our home. My wife and I always kiss three times and have passed that on to the boys as well. Zero kisses was the trademark in my home growing up, so to be able to do that when Dad couldn't object felt right. To my surprise, Dad received each kiss warmly as if he had been waiting for them.

"I love you," I told my dad for the first time in my life, at forty-seven years old—again, knowing Dad couldn't object and partially that hoping sleep had taken him away and he hadn't heard me.

"I love you too, Kev." Dad pushed another forty-seven-year first.

We both needed that, and with those five words, I was at peace with knowing the end wasn't far away.

At 9:30 a.m. on April 2, I got the call from Lisa that I was dreading and expecting. Dad had passed away; no more light would pass through his eyes.

Just two nights before, I had sat by Dad's bedside while he slept in his hospice room and I read from this book. I read the first few chapters because I knew Dad had never read my book. In the last several years, reading had become very frustrating for Dad because his mind couldn't focus. I understood he wanted to read the book, but he just couldn't. We had talked about the book a lot over the last five years since it had been published. We had talked about the impact of the life we had lived. We had talked about the give and take that came with being a multicultural/transracial family. We had talked about the pressure put on a multicultural family, and we had talked about his regrets as a father of a multicultural family.

We struggled with where we would fit in and feel at home. When we lived in the black neighborhood, it was often a hellish experience for my brothers, who were picked on because they were the minority. When we moved to the white neighborhood, I occasionally felt the same type of hell my brothers endured, often feeling uncomfortable and targeted because I was the minority. It was that pressure on our family that created what began as a hairline fracture and over the years grew to what at times felt like a Grand Canyon–sized gap in our family. My dad regretted that as the head of our home, he didn't know how to pull us back together. My sister, my mother, and I have remained close. The pressure of being a conspicuous family has soldered us together instead of tearing us apart. I wish I could say the same about my relationship with my two brothers.

The retelling of our story, which I saw as a wonderful experience, opened old wounds for two of my three siblings. Being too caught up in my own experience, I failed to recognize their experiences and just how difficult life must have been for them. In grade school and high school, they were often the minorities, and being the minority in any situation is a challenge. I should have understood that and validated their experiences and their challenges more in the book's first edition. Brothers can have regrets too.

In recognizing their experience, I have to concede to some possible truths. It is my assumption that their belief is that our family made a lot of concessions for the darker-skinned family member, concessions that caused my brothers to sacrifice over and over. Those sacrifices came at a cost, and the investments had little to no return for my brothers, in their eyes. I could be way off on this assumption, but I have no way of knowing because we don't talk, much less talk about the tough issues that came with being a transracial family.

There are some truths to those thoughts. My parents did make a lot of concessions for me. We moved to a black neighborhood, which benefited me, but it wasn't done solely for me. Their thought was that we could all benefit from living around people different from us. Unfortunately, the motivation behind why we moved to Detroit was never discussed.

If that is how they feel, I understand it. As children in a transracial family, they were left out of many, many decisions. As an adoptee, I was also left out of many, many decisions. As children in general, we were left out of many, many decisions. Making the decisions wasn't where my parents went wrong. It was making the decisions without giving explanations; that caused us to make a left when we should have gone right.

In my parents' defense, they didn't have a road map to follow. Transracial adoption was such a new and unusual concept in the late sixties and early seventies. There was no one going before them leaving breadcrumbs, so naturally they made some mistakes.

It is from those mistakes and oversights that I write this addition to the book. Over the five years since the book was originally published, I have come across so much I wanted to address and so much more instruction I needed to leave. I realized I had plenty of breadcrumbs to place to help the families like ours find their way and avoid the fractures and breaks that we have experienced. The lessons learned and instruction can be summarized in three areas: family, race and identity, and advocacy. In each section I will address some key things I have learned and give action plans for transracial families to help you avoid the mistakes and the pitfalls that come with such a unique lifestyle.

WHEN PEOPLE SHOW YOU WHO THEY ARE: CREATING BALANCE AND AVOIDING INVISIBLE CHILDREN

How did we miss it? How did we not see that the experiences of all the children in our family were valid and needed to be heard? It was missed because my needs seemed more immediate. It was missed because my siblings' needs weren't as obvious, and the busyness of life hid them. In a family of six, we weren't digging and looking for additional challenges. There was plenty to deal with on the surface.

For a multicultural family, part of the challenge is not knowing where to dig. The soil underneath my brothers and sister was rich yet compacted and hard from neglect. Having the advantage of additional knowledge and time, it is easy to see each one of us would be affected in some way by this unique family makeup.

My siblings should have been given the freedom to voice their experiences. It should have been anticipated that they would have some issues, and there should have been an action plan in place to address, unearth, and dust off those issues. My parents had both the curse and the blessing that came with being pioneers in transracial adoption. The curse was that we didn't even know digging was necessary. The blessing was that for decades, we remained blissfully ignorant to the effects of such a life, if that is a blessing. Now as adults, we are trying to piece together a family that didn't understand the pressure of a transracial life. We are trying to pull together a family that is splintered by resentment, anger, hurt, confusion, frustration, and bitterness, and even with the most herculean effort, some pieces of the puzzle may be too worn to fit back together.

Over the years as the gap between my brothers and me grew larger and larger, I spun a cocoon around my heart, lying to myself and insisting I didn't need them. This is a skill I have learned to perfect as part of my adoption residue. The fear of being hurt in relationships enacts a protective mechanism in me that simply severs the relationship. I cut the tie with my brothers, convincing myself I didn't need them. The severing of this bond then began erasing the fond memories I had and the relationships I had built with my brothers as we grew up. I pushed the closeness we once shared, the games we played, and the connections we had back into a seldom-used corner of my mind.

Then Dad died, and I had to share space with them as we all convened at Mom's (formerly Mom and Dad's) house over Easter in anticipation of the funeral. Only then did I see the brothers I grew up with that I had forgotten. I saw the sense of humor and shocking honestly that my oldest brother possesses and that I have always admired. I saw the kind qualities in my other brother, which helped me to remember that we were at one time best friends. I also still saw the pain that he carried that caused him to push so many away. It was then that I had to honestly say I missed them. I missed them being in my life. I missed being a part of my nieces' and nephews' lives, and I hated the fact that I didn't know them now.

My parents were in many ways decades ahead of the curve. They understood I was a special-needs adoption. As a child of a different race, I did have very specific and special needs, and my parents made sure that I was surrounded by friends, peers, and families who looked like me. That was life changing for me, but at the same time it was life challenging for my brothers. While I walked through life, in many instances stride for stride with children of color who understood what my life experience was, my brothers didn't have that same benefit. Their white friends were few and far between.

Being a minority in any situation is not easy, and it is especially difficult for adolescents, who expend so much energy on just being part of the group. I am not saying that they couldn't or didn't have close friendships with black children because they did, but to have close friends who experience life as you do is different, especially in a city like Detroit, which was so defined and outlined by race.

My brothers too had the added questions that if and when they did have white friends, how would they to respond if their white friends didn't embrace people of color? Was it their job to speak out against racism even if it meant losing a friend in an environment where friendships were sparse? If they didn't speak up, how would they deal with the guilt that may come from not speaking up for a family member? If they didn't speak up, how would they keep the secret that their brother is black?

The stress of being a conspicuous family carries its own weight, and there are times when you just want to "be" as a child; you just want to blend in and be like every other kid. The membership in the transracial community means blending in is no longer an option.

It was great that my parents understood I was a special-needs adoption and went to great lengths to make sure my needs were met. But my siblings also had special needs, and they should have been celebrated. Instead, it is easy to see why my brothers may have felt invisible. There was so much energy put into making sure my needs were met that my brothers' needs appeared to have been overlooked.

Striking the right balance in the transracial family is important and will not happen organically. The life of a transracial family must be purposeful, proactive, and progressive. You must anticipate the needs of all the children and act to make sure everyone's needs are met. You must be willing to change and adapt as your children change and adapt.

Action Items for Families

1. Make a list of the anticipated needs of all your children, and create a measureable plan to address the needs. For example, one of the anticipated needs of my brothers should have been their need to just be an inconspicuous family. We could have addressed this by creating date night with Mom and/or Dad, to go out alone and connect and be inconspicuous.

2. Create a tradition centered on the culture and race of your biological children. Create a tradition centered on the culture of your adoptive children. Create a tradition centered on the culture of your multicultural family. Give everyone the space to express and celebrate who they are as parts of the family and as individuals. An example of this could be that you research and cook with each family member a meal from their specific culture. Then you create a meal that combines different foods from each culture, and it becomes a celebrated meal in your multicultural home.

3. Take time to sit and talk with your biological children and adoptive children about their experiences as children in your multicultural family. Let them know they are heard and seen.

WHEN PEOPLE SHOW YOU WHO THEY ARE—BELIEVE THEM AND ADJUST ACCORDINGLY

As Maya Angelou said, "When people show you who they are, believe them."

It is painful for me to picture that fall day when my brothers played with my grandfather in a way I never did. What hurts even more is to understand how I internalized it. Unfortunately, my grandparents very subtly and most likely unconsciously supported the running tape in my head that kept telling me I wasn't worthy. How could I be worthy when my own mother gave me away? So, naturally I thought my grandparents weren't as comfortable around me because something was off with me.

Parents, understand that there will be people in your life who will struggle with your decision to adopt transracially. My grandparents showed us who they were many times, and my mother and father knew it. It is your job as parents to protect your children first. Just as you wouldn't allow a pedophile around your child for fear that they would harm your child, you must also contain contact with those like my grandparents. Understand that even though my parents did contain the contact I had with my grandparents, I still walked away feeling less than. Please hear that.

Don't assume limited contact will erase the problem totally. When and if your children are around people you feel are questionable, be sure to protect them while in contact and debrief and lift them up after the contact. I needed someone to help me sort out the uneasiness I had with my grandparents. I needed someone to help me to see that it wasn't me—it was them. I needed someone to simply explain the background my grandparents came from and how that affected them. I needed to understand that the changes my grandparents were making, although far from perfect, were a huge stretch for them, and realistically it wasn't in them to stretch any further. Having that conversation about the possibility that my grandparents' shortcomings may have been why we didn't exactly mesh would have caused me to walk taller.

It is your responsibility to frame these difficult but necessary conversations with your children. Please don't assume that if your child feels uneasy, he or she will come to you. Be purposeful, proactive, and progressive. As the adult you have to begin these conversations.

Blunt and honest conversations with family and friends are also your responsibility. Obviously, my parents should have had a very open and honest conversation with my grandparents. In the conversation, it should have been explained what would be accepted and what wouldn't be accepted prior to me becoming part of the family.

Understand that not everyone will be in line with your commitment to diversity, and some will react negatively to your decision to adopt transracially. As you become more fused as a multicultural family, your understanding of the world and the impact of color in the world may and should change. As your views change, so might and should your circle of friends. Your circle may and should go through a "tanning process." As color impacts your life, the need to have others in your circle who understand a colorized world should increase. Please make sure your child is not your only symbol of diversity in your circle. If you are considering adopting children of color, the colorization of your circle should begin before your child comes home.

The number of people of color in your circle should increase, which will be beneficial to you and your children of color.

Action Items for Parents
1. Write a letter to or have a conversation with your extended family about the fact that your family has changed. Understand the expectations around your family must change as well. The racial jokes at the Thanksgiving table will no longer be tolerated. The jokes about the damaged adoptee at the Fourth of July picnic need to stop.
2. Find the patriarchs and matriarchs of the family. Ask them to help with this message. Having them set the tone for the family can be very powerful. Oftentimes many in the family with follow the lead of those patriarchs and matriarchs.
3. Create a plan of containment. There are some family members or friends who will not change. You know who they are! How do you contain their contact with your

children to protect your children? It may not mean total containment. It may mean simply that you don't allow your children to be alone with them, and when there is contact it should be followed up with a debrief with your adoptee.

4. Explore how your transracial adoptee views your family and friends. It is as simple as asking, "What do you think of Uncle Herman? Is he nice to you?" Children can be very honest, and if they give you any indication that they aren't comfortable around Uncle Herman, explore those feelings and adjust accordingly.

MY PROCESS. MY STORY. MY WORDS.

Very often many like to split adoptees into two different camps: the angry/bitter adoptees versus the naïve/grateful adoptees. What I've found is that it isn't that simple; we aren't that simple. There are days when I could be categorized as living in both camps. Yes, I can be grateful that I was adopted because life in my birth family would not have been good for me, and I can be bitter and angry that I was denied the opportunity to meet my birth mother before she died. I've matured enough to know I can be both or one or the other, and that is all right.

I have also had to learn that my experience isn't every adoptee's experience, and I am not speaking for the adoptee community. We adoptees don't think the same, feel the same, or experience life the same. This is important because what I speak on will not apply to every adoptee, but my hope is what I share will bring a better understanding of some of the issues and challenges your children may face.

This process is fluid, not static, and it changes, ebbs, and flows, and that is all right too. I am fifty years old now, and the process still isn't done for me. The thought that children are resilient and will just "get over" everything that comes with adoption simply isn't true. Adoption and all that comes with it don't stop with a judge's signature.

Parents, understand that about your adopted children. Their feelings about adoption and all that come with it can be one thing today and something totally different tomorrow. Give your children the freedom to float on top of the waves that come with the emotions behind adoption, and support them. Sit with them, and hold them above water while they figure out the complexities that come with this life.

As an adoptee, I know that regardless of how dark and clouded my story is, it is my story. I am the proud product of a relationship that occurred between my white mother and black father while they were still married...to other people. Although being proud of being created out of adultery makes many pause, it is my story. The peace that comes with the truth overrides the shame of adultery for me.

What is your child's story? What have you told him or her about it? When (not if) you tell his or her story, be truthful at an age-appropriate level. Resist the overwhelming urge to fill in the blanks with fantasy or untruths. If there are parts of the story you don't know, say that. Resist the urge to fix the pain you can't. Holding your child while he or she sits with this history may be all you can offer. Learn to be quiet in the uncomfortable moments. What makes you pause may strangely be a source of pride for your child, something he or she holds dear because it is his or hers.

"What if we don't know anything about their story?" you might ask.

The same rules apply; be truthful, don't backfill with fairy tales, and sit still.

Lastly, understand that so much about adoption comes down to control for many adoptees. Most likely they haven't had much control over this process of adoption to this point. One way to give adoptees some control back is to give them control over their stories.

People will want to know their stories and will ask and pry and plead to know the intimate details. Let your child know he or she ultimately controls when it's heard and who gets to hear it.

"My daughter loves telling her third-grade classmates why she was put in foster care, and trust me, her story isn't pretty," a concerned adoptive mother recently told me. "She doesn't have much of a filter, and I am concerned her classmates will judge her because of her story."

She's right. They may judge her daughter. But what makes the mother and others cringe is a thread taken from her daughter's tapestry. A thread she may hold dear. It is a piece of what makes up her daughter. Instead of not letting her tell the story, I suggested the mother work with her daughter to say the same thing in a different way. I cautioned her to not become the sole editor of her daughter's story, but to work with her daughter on the edits and be willing to concede some of the narrative.

Parents, it is also your responsibility to frame the conversation of adoption, and to reframe the conversation when it leans to the "savior" topic. This can easily be done by making things clear when people praise you for your charitable act of adoption. You can simply say, "This child has saved us in ways you can't comprehend. What this child brings to this family cannot be measured. This child wasn't the one who needed saving!" Use this as an opportunity to build up your children instead of allowing them to feel obligated to you. Be prepared to respond when the questions come up.

"When I was growing up, my dad used to talk to the TV. We would sit in the front room, and he would literally talk to the TV," my good friend Bill told me. "He would have these deep political, racial, and moral debates with the TV. It wasn't until after my dad passed away when I was an adult that I realized my dad wasn't talking to the TV—he was talking to me through the TV!" Bill excitedly shared his "ah-ha" moment.

When people approach you in the grocery store and ask you horribly insensitive and personal things about your children, their history, or their adoption in front of them, realize this is an opportunity for you. This is an opportunity to talk to your child through the person who stands next you in the cereal aisle, in the same way Bill's dad talked to him through the TV. Use this time wisely! Use this time to build them up, teach them adoption is not something shameful, and give them the words to speak later in life. Model for them how to respond, so when they get older they will be comfortable and able to respond to similar questions.

As they get older and the questions continue, you can turn to them and ask them if they feel comfortable sharing their stories in front of the Apple Jacks.

Action Items for Parents

1. Write out what you know of your child's story, and then review it. If you haven't shared it with your child, do so, but first consider the following questions: Is it age appropriate? Is it truthful? Does your description honor your child's story? Rewrite it until you can answer yes to all three.

2. In the next week, share your child's story with him or her if you haven't to this point. If you have talked about it before, make sure to readdress it with the points above. Be clear with your child that this is his or her story, and he or she has control over who gets to hear it, when it gets shared, and where it gets shared. Keep in mind that your child may be receptive and interested in hearing it or not. This doesn't mean it will be that way forever. Respect your child's process and come back to it later

3. Create a response to the scenario below:

   You are in the grocery store with your adopted children (for some reason people love to approach transracial families in the grocery store and say some horribly inappropriate things—*beware!*), and a friend walks up to you and says, "You know, I got to tell you I admire you so much for what you are doing for these kids. You should be up for sainthood."

   Create a response that lifts up your children, and store it away so when you are in the produce section and confronted with this comment, you can respond in a way that sends a strong message to your child. Remember you are talking to your child, not the inquisitive mind who wants to know.

Search and Reunion

Friday night, October 30, 2009, I took my boys to the local high school football game. It was my youngest son's big night to be a part of the high school game. He got to eat dinner in the high school with his teammates from the third-and-fourth-grade football team. Then they got to go on the field and cheer the big high school players as they ran out on the field. To my nine-year-old, this was like getting to see a professional football team up close. To him these guys were bigger and stronger than anyone he had ever seen. It was great to see him so excited about being part of the game.

His older brother went to socialize and study the female species.

Earlier in the day, I had been online having a discussion with another adoptee about searching for her birth parents. She told me she had been able to find them and her siblings relatively easily. I mentioned that I was interested in starting up my search for my birth mother again and asked her where I should start. My fellow adoptee referred me to her adoption angel, Cher; an adoption angel is someone who searches for birth parents and adoptees on a volunteer basis. Before I could respond, I got an e-mail back from my fellow adoptee stating she had spoken with Cher and told Cher I would be contacting her. On my way out to the football game, I sent Cher, now my adoption angel, a message.

In the e-mail I advised Cher I was looking for my birth mother. I gave her what I believed to be my birth mother's last name, my date of birth, and my place of birth.

The high school stadium was a five-to-eight-minute drive away from our house. By the time I was in my seat at the football game, my phone was buzzing. I had received an e-mail from Cher, and she had additional questions. Answering the questions, I quickly hit send and was getting excited about the possibilities. Cher sent an e-mail back in the next five minutes stating she had found a possible match.

Immediately, Cher asked a few more questions in another e-mail. Cher wanted to know if I knew of any other children my birth mother may have had. I rocketed back to her that I knew my birth mother had children—three or four children, and I knew one was a girl. Cher was able to find three boys associated with a woman she thought was my birth mother immediately.

My heart was pounding now, and the loud football game twenty yards in front of me was a distant sound I could barely hear.

More questions and answers flew back and forth. Each answer narrowed the search, and the possible became more probable. Cher told me she was confident she had found my birth mother. As she dug deeper and deeper, Cher found an obituary. My birth mother had passed away in 2003.

The football game that surrounded me went quiet. My internal response to this news was small. A few years ago, when thinking over the idea of looking for my birth mother, I had contemplated and accepted that one outcome could be that she may have passed away. The news was not shocking, and internally it was as if I had already known.

In her death came the last puzzle piece. In the obituary it showed she was survived by three sons and one daughter. The presence of a daughter brought us even closer. Cher wanted to know if I knew the ages of the children when I was born. Off the top of my head, I didn't know, but I knew that at home, my nonindentifying paperwork sent to me by the adoption agency in 1988 showed each child's age. Once we knew their ages, we could match and pretty much confirm whether this was my birth mother and her family.

It was only the second quarter of the football game, and I had to wait until the game was over to go home. The game was a blowout, but both of my sons were off with their friends somewhere in the crowd. I knew how much they enjoyed the Friday-night lights, more for social reasons than football. We stayed for two more quarters in the rain, and it felt like the time on the scoreboard was going backward.

The game finally ended, and I raced home to find my paperwork. I e-mailed it to Cher. It was confirmed. The ages on my paperwork of my siblings matched the information Cher had found.

Cher was sending e-mail after e-mail in rapid-fire mode, and it was hard to keep up with, but I was happy. By this time, I was starved for more information, and Cher continued to shovel to me forkful after forkful.

In the assault of information, I got names of three brothers and one sister, the location of the cemetery where my birth mother was buried, pictures of the cemetery, and pictures of my birth mother's headstone. The last pieces of information were my sister's address and phone number. Cher suggested I call my sister to see what she knew. It was close to 11:00 p.m., and the conversation with my sister would have to wait until the morning.

My wife, Shilease, had come home by this time, and we read through the e-mails again together. We both sat in my office, quiet, occasionally remarking on how unbelievable all this new information was to us.

My calm, reasoning side tried to convince my excited emotional side that this was not my birth mother. Shilease and I went over the information and compared it to that from the agency in my nonidentifying-information letter.

The woman we found had the same last name as the last name confirmed by the agency years ago. This woman's age; the fact that she lived close to Detroit, where I was born; the number of children; and the sexes of the children all coincided with the information I had in my letter. The odds of this not being the woman were astronomical. Reason lost to logic and the hopes of my emotional side. This was my mother, and I had missed her by six years.

I wrote the above eight years ago when looking for and finally finding my birth mother, Helen. There was so much I learned from that experience and my eight years of processing it. I was able to finally meet my sister and one brother. The other two brothers had no interest in meeting me. I also spoke to my mother's husband. That was a very interesting conversation, and he was the one who finally put me in touch with my sister...who had been looking for me. To know that someone was looking for me filled my heart. To know someone knew about me and wanted to find me partially filled my Helen-sized hole.

I stayed in contact with me sister and brother for a few years, and then we drifted apart. I have watched so many reunion shows where the adoptee and birthmother meet and everyone is crying, including me. They are usually filled with hugs and resolution. What I found was that no one tells you how to maintain those relationships *after* the reunion. It is especially hard when you are an adult adoptee, and the only connection you share is DNA.

Soon after the reunion, the word spread that I had been found, and person after person reached out to me via Facebook. It got to the point where I couldn't keep track of who was who and how we are related. I think a large part of the interest was the story. Everyone wanted to see the result of the affair Helen had had, and some hadn't previously even been aware she had had an affair. So I was this oddity, and after a while I felt like a sideshow. On top of that I began to feel like my sister wanted me to fix the deficiencies in the family. I was a link to the mother she didn't really know. It became very obvious early on that their family functioned on a high level of dysfunction. It was also very evident that I, as a child of color, would not have fared well with my mother's husband, who was at best only verbally abusive to my mother and their children. That is why I stated earlier that my parents' decision to adopt was the right decision for me.

The family was so dysfunctional that my sister left when she was fourteen and never really developed a relationship with our mother. So when I came along, I felt like she wanted me to glue everyone back together. After a while it became too overwhelming, and I decided for my well-being I had to distance myself from the family.

I want to be clear that although we didn't have a storybook ending, I needed to connect with the family. I needed to have a lot of questions answered, and when I got what I needed, I was fine with it. I have no regrets and am happy I was able to make the connections. I strongly feel all adoptive families should be open to and assist in the search and reunion. My parents were very open to it and were actually there when I met my sister for the first time. Honestly, I needed their support and was relieved they were so open to helping and finding answers.

Lastly, I never mourned the death of my mother because I never was connected to her emotionally. My parents never talked about her when I was a child, although I thought a lot about her. Growing up, I needed to know it was OK to talk about my birth mother. I needed to express my thoughts and process my feelings about it. Since that never happened, I never grew roots that connected me to her. When I found out she had passed away, I felt nothing, and I can't help but feel guilty about that. We should have given more honor to her, and I should have been allowed to explore all that I was feeling.

Action Items for parents

1) Find a way to honor the birth family *no matter what.* I understand some children come from horrible beginnings, but the bottom line is, no matter how they came to you, without the birth family, you wouldn't have your child. So how do you honor the family? Some adoptive parents make a point to celebrate the birth family and take time out to thank them for their sacrifice on special days like the child's birthday. Some families make it a point to pray for the birth family every night.

   Find a way to honor them, and understand that by honoring and showing love to the birth family, you are really teaching your children how to honor and love *you.*

2) Don't wait for your child to bring up his or her birth family. Don't fall prey to the temptation that says, "When our child is ready, they will come to us and ask questions." That shouldn't be your child's responsibility. You must initiate the conversation. It can be as simple as asking if your child thinks about his or her birth family and letting him or her know that you do too.

3) One time it not enough. If you approach the topic and your child seems uninterested, leave it alone for now, but revisit it in a few months, even if you have to set a date on

your calendar in three to six months to bring it up again.

4) Make it clear you will help your child search if you don't know who the birth family is. Beware of the romanticism that comes with searching. Oftentimes chasing and solving the puzzle become more attractive than the final outcome. Understand the emotion that goes into it, which may mean your child wants to search today but not tomorrow and not for six months. Remember that he or she is steering this train—you're just along for the ride. Your child gets to set the pace.

5) If your child is on social media, please be sure his or her identity is protected and security settings are activated. We want to prevent someone connecting with your child before he or she is ready.

6) If you don't have any information on your child's birth family yet and he or she shows a desire to find them, consider doing DNA testing to give your child some background and a sense of his or her genealogy. Ancestry. com and 23 and Me are two services you can explore.

Adoption Residue

"Boy, that Helen did a number on you!" my wife will often tease me.

Helen, my birthmother, did do a number on me, and it has taken me years to recognize this simple truth. As I look at it now, I wonder why I ever thought I wouldn't be affected by this separation. For decades I have chased, stalked, and pursued ways to fill the Helen-sized hole in my heart, a hole that was created in August of 1967 when Helen and I parted ways.

For me, I hunted for Helen in relationships—in familial relationships, peer relationships, and dating relationships. I hoped to find the balm that would heal my primal wound. I looked for approval by being the good son, the loyal friend, and the womanizer.

Although I hate the expectation that adoptees should be grateful, I think I wore that expectation like a tailored suit. I sought to get good grades but was derailed early when a teacher convinced me I was not a bright child. For the most part I was a good kid who took pride in not causing my parents any additional trouble. My desire to be the good son compelled me to stay at Alma College 4 years longer than I should have stayed.

Friendships weren't always easy because I was very guarded. I was horribly shy until I got to know someone. If I found someone willing to walk through the tall grass of my insecurities, I was loyal to a fault. I was also fortunate that I was surrounded by a good group of kids. If I hadn't been, the siren's call may have lured me into a different way of life. My loyalty to friends could have caused me to make some poor choices in exchange for being liked by my peers.

As I set out to date in my midteens, I looked for women to calm the burn created from my separation from Helen. My mother can tell you there were many days and nights I was brokenhearted because the woman I was dating didn't fit into Helen's wound.

When I did find a girl who was of substance, I struggled to be faithful because I feared the young lady would leave me, and I would be left alone. Dating became a competition for me as to who could hurt the other first because the pain was inevitable. I struggled to manage those relationships, and what I was looking for in those girls I would never find. Now I know I entered those relationships doomed, and the stress and strife I caused those girls and myself was unavoidable. In many instances, I would have been better off alone, but the thought of being alone terrified me. Often I chose to be in relationship with someone totally wrong for me, and I was totally wrong for her. I did that because I thought an incompatible relationship was better than none at all. I moved from relationship to relationship, hoping the next girl could quiet the voices in my head that told me I wasn't worthy of a relationship. Unfortunately, I entered into many relationships I never should have, and of course they failed. This only reinforced what the voices in my head were saying. It was a vicious mouse wheel I got on, and it took me years to step off.

I have coined the term "adoption residue," which is the stuff that comes with adoption that we can't simply wash off. As I described above, my struggles with self-esteem and relationships are my most obvious adoption residue. Now that I know that, I can navigate around those pitfalls that I fell into so easily over and over.

As I have stated, adoptees are not one size fits all, so my big issues may not be your adoptee's residue, but understand all adoptees has some residue. Also understand it can be both positive and negative. I responded to the feeling of being unworthy by self-sabotaging my attempts to succeed. Another adoptee may respond to this by being very driven, which can materialize in great success. My hope is that if we understand the presence of the primal wound, then parents can look for ways to soothe the pain that for many has been unidentified to this point.

Action Items for Parents
1) How do you think your child responds to the primal wound? Look for an area where he or she struggles, and see if it may be related to this wound. Have a conversation about that area with your child. If you don't know how to resolve it, sometimes just pointing it out can bring about positive changes for him or her.
2) Find ways to show your child that he or she is wonderful beyond measure. Encourage your child in the areas your child excels, and speak life into him or her. Find others whom your child respects, and work with them to also speak life into your child.

Find mentors who look like your child and who can help amplify how amazing your child is and show your child that he or she can grow up to be amazing too.

LIVING IN RACIAL ISOLATION

The first edition of this book has been used as a text book for a class on multiculturalism at Lordes University in Toledo Ohio. Once a semester I visit the classes and I share from my experience as a transracial adoptee and the students ask questions about my life. I enjoy it and learn so much from the minds of young people.

In one class the idea of racial isolation came up. I was explaining that a large majority of transracial adoptees live their lives in racial isolation, rarely seeing anyone that looks like them. One white student spoke shared that in his predominately white high school there was one black student. He went on to say that from his point of view the black student seemed to do fine in this environment.

I explained that the burden of being the "only one" weighs heavy on you. Most don't realize the stress that comes with being the only one. I challenged the white student to reach out to his black classmate and ask him what his experience was like in high school.

A few days later, I got an email for the white student. It read, "Thanks for explaining what racial isolation is in class. I was able to reach my classmate and we had a long talk about his high school experience. He shared with me the struggles he had that I was blind to. We had a good talked and he appreciated the fact that I took the time to hear what his life was like."

Parents, have you ever been in a situation where you are the only one? Have you ever been in a large group where there were no other white people? How did that feel? Consider that this may be your child's daily experience and how that must feel. The weight of being the only one every day, all day, will cause the strongest shoulders to bow.

My parents gave me access to role models, peers, and their families who looked like me, and it was there where the seeds of my racial identity were planted.

The life of a multicultural family is purposeful. It is an ever-evolving mission of finding ways to celebrate all the cultures and races represented in your family. What are you doing on a consistent basis to put your children in touch with kids who look like them?

My parents had the luxury of being able to simply say, "Go out and play," and that is how I was put in contact with kids who looked like me. If that is not your situation, you have to understand your "Go out and play" will include some windshield time. You will have to seek out venues like athletic leagues, dance troops, dance classes, chess clubs, et cetera, that are composed of mostly children who look like your son or daughter.

If you adopted a child who had a special need, and his or her therapist was across town, but you knew taking your child to the therapist three times a week would be a benefit, would you do it? Of course you would.

It has to be the same type of commitment with transracial adoption. Your child of color has a special need—to be in connection with people who look like him or her.

Get on the Internet, and find the "therapy" your child needs; ask people of color; tackle someone in a grocery store if you have to. Do what you must. The connection I had allowed me to grow up to be proud of my skin color instead of ashamed of it. The connections that Sara lacked put the burden on her to figure things out—as she stated, an unfair burden to put on a child.

Action Item for Parents
1. Search the Internet for local cultural events like those around the Martin Luther King Day celebration, Cinqo de Mayo, et cetera. Go and *talk* to people. Be up front and honest. Let them know you are raising a child of color and that you understand the importance of putting your child in contact with people who look like him or her. Ask for suggestions as to how you can do that and what groups are out there, and then follow up, exchange numbers, and remember you are one connection away from changing your child's life.
2. Design a therapy plan for your adoptee. Come up with ways to get your child that connection. Look into opportunities like Big Brothers, Big Sisters, and find sports leagues, dance troops, cheerleading groups, et cetera.

BLACK WITH HUES

I look back fondly at the Whitcomb neighborhood and the cast of characters I called my friends. I learned so much from them, and besides all the craziness, it was an important time for me. In this neighborhood, I learned that black is three dimensional.

If I didn't have this early exposure to black people, I think my view of the black community would be so different. I grew up in a time when the only representation of blacks on TV were the sorry two-dimensional characters created by white people. There was Fred Sanford, the jive-talking junk man; JJ Evans, the jive-talking son and brother from the Evans family; and George Jefferson, the jive-talking owner of several dry-cleaning business—"one near you." They were all the same character with different names. I was fortunate that I grew up seeing there was so much more to black than Fred, JJ, and George.

I had nice black friends and mean black friends. I had generous black friends and not-so-generous black friends. In their presentation of black, they showed me a black that I wanted to be a part of, and they helped to create a positive racial identity in me—so much so that I remember feeling bad for my brothers and sister because they weren't black. I was so proud to be a part of that community, and never once did I wish I was anything else but black.

I often hear some transracial families or adoptees share that they really struggled with this growing up. This move to Detroit gave me so much. It gave me a steady foundation to build my racial identity, and it is the thing I am most thankful for having as I grew up.

The collision of adoption and discrimination can send some very damaging messages to transracial adoptees. As an adoptee, I struggled with thoughts of being worthy because, for whatever reason, my mother gave me away, and I reasoned a child who is given away can't be worth too much. When you mix in racial discrimination, the combined effects can be potent.

During adolescence I began to feel the weight of discrimination and racism. I heard the messages loud and clear that I and people like me were considered less than. But my lighthouse was the everyday black people I saw and came in contact with who pointed my identity in a positive direction. As my identity was pointed in the right direction, being comfortable in my skin cushioned the blows that came with the discrimination and racism.

My friends showed me that being black was a wonderful life to live. They were my superheroes, and I couldn't wait to grow up and wear the cape that came with being black.

Action Items for Parents

1. Create a plan to show your child the many hues of who he or she is as a child of color. Search out those "lighthouses" who will help in the development of your child's racial identity.

   Does your child have access to toys, magazines, books, and movies that represent him or her? Do you have people who look like your child coming in and out of your home? What message is sent to your child if your home is absent of images and people who look like him or her? Remember, the life of a transracial family is purposeful. Be proactive in the messages and images you send your child of color.

2. Although things are better today than when I grew up, it is still important to show your child the many hues of who he or she is as a child of color. You can do this by finding professionals who look like him or her. So seek out doctors who look like your child, connect with organizations that center around pride in that community, and ask for a list of professionals you can reach out to and include in your tanning community.

3. One of your biggest jobs as a parent of a child of color is that you must balance the scales. Society and the media do a wonderful job of driving home the message that people of color are less than (research the Clark Doll test). It is your job to balance out those messages by feeding your child with positive message about who he or she is and about the group he or she comes from.

   Some of the biggest message providers are our school systems. Our school systems do a very poor job of showing the contributions of people of color. Teach your children there are more historical figures that look like them than Martin Luther King Jr., Eli Whitney, George Washington Carver, and President Barack Obama. As a purposeful parent, you will have to supplement their educations to show them they are more than slaves or hired help. You will be amazed to see the stories that aren't told about people of color. Your children will walk taller when they learn the giants they have come from.

"OTHERING" AND MICROAGGRESSIONS

I reread the chapter that talks about us moving from the black neighborhood to the white neighborhood and my introduction to being treated like a minority. There is so much I would tell the young, unsure Kevin. There was so much I just walked into without knowing how to decipher. That was too much for a child at eight years old to take in at once.

I had to learn a new neighborhood, meet new friends, and at the same time digest being "othered." So much of what I write about in this section is the uncomfortable feeling of being pointed out as different, or being "othered." To this day I detest that feeling.

As an adoptee and an adolescent, I just wanted to be like every other child in the neighborhood. I just wanted to blend in, but in the middle of my first game of Ditch It, it was obvious that wasn't going to happen. As I stated, the children in this neighborhood were left to figure out how to get along. Although we eventually did, it came at the expense of one. It was assumed that I should learn to just deal with it because I was not the norm. It didn't crush me, and I learned to deal with it, but there were shots to my self-esteem that I shouldn't have had to endure. The inadequate feelings I had about myself were supported over and over again by this type of treatment

It was the more causal slights that I didn't know how to quantify. So I walked away many times, as I did with Grandma and Grandpa, feeling as though I was defective. How could I not? So many people around me were telling me and showing me the same thing.

Oftentimes when I speak with transracial families, many assume that if they can just find a diverse neighborhood to live in, their children will be safe. The misconception is that with diversity comes understanding. It is assumed that if we put people of different cultures and races together, they will learn from each other through osmosis. So if I merely live next to a gay couple, I will learn through the walls how to be respectful of all gays. That's ridiculous.

It's even more naïve to think kids can figure it out. Most adults I know aren't sure how to respect and honor different races and cultures, yet we give that job to children in these diverse spaces and expect them to figure it out.

It's your job as parents to help your children and those around them manage the diversity. It should be painfully obvious by now, but I will state it again: your children shouldn't *be* the diversity in every circle they are a part of. Diversity is a wonderful thing, but it must be guided, so everyone is respected.

Learning how to navigate this new space and understanding race and racism can seem overwhelming. It was the microaggressions and subtle slights that confused me and made me question myself. The obvious, crystal-clear racism was easier to deal with because there was no question what was happening in those incidents. As parents of children of color, you will have to learn to tune in to a new frequency. As you become more experienced, you will be better able to hear the chatter on the microaggression stations. It will become natural to notice when things hit you and just don't feel right. When they do, you have to be ready to address them.

Action Items for Families

1. What is being done in the circles that your children move in to assure they are being respected and not othered? Read chapter 6, "Promoted," with your children and ask them if they ever feel like I did. Let them know that when it happens, they can come to you, so you can work together to make sure it doesn't happen again. If you become aware of an incident that makes them feel othered, talk to your children about it *before* you act. Let them be in on the resolution. By doing so you will teach them how to speak up and resolve things on their own someday.

2. Understand that with microaggressions, intention has nothing to do with effect. As the need arises for you to advocate for your child, don't get lured into the trap of arguing the offender's intention. If you child has been put in a position to feel slighted or othered, the offending person's intentions have nothing to do with your child's feelings. Save this definition to refer back to when needed. Later I will talk more about advocating for your children when incidents arise.

CODE-SWITCHING

When I reread this book, a few things jumped out at me that I no longer believe. I made a statement about me learning black culture through osmosis. That may be poetic and romantic, but I didn't learn about black culture through osmosis. The understanding of cultural rules didn't magically seep through my skin. I lived a very purposeful life. As I came to the realization that I was seen as a child of color, I knew I would have to cling to that group for social survival, so my actions were very purposeful to assure my acceptance into this group. I studied, watched, learned, and crammed at times to get all I could get of black culture. I understood there was a gap in my knowledge of black culture. There was so much about black culture I wanted to know and simply didn't have access to at home.

I became a student, and I would sit and listen and become aware of expected speech patterns and beliefs in black culture. As I grew, I understood this could be different, very different, between cultures. So I watched and learned and studied differences, so I knew what were expected speech patterns and beliefs in white culture as well.

This was exhausting at times, especially when I was younger. But today it is one of my most valued skills. The mastery or inability to shift between patterns often meant the difference between inclusion and exclusion. The technical term for what I was doing is "code-switching," which *Merriam-Webster* defines as "the switching from the linguistic system of one language or dialect to that of another."

It is a way that different cultures distinguish whether you belong or not. It can be regional or generational, and knowing when and where to use each pattern is important.

So I learned to talk one way with my black friends and one way with my white friends, and after a while the switching back and forth become unconscious. It is not forced, and not much thought is put into it now. There is a familiarity and closeness that comes from being with a group that communicates in a way that is unique.

The ability to code switch helped me gain entrance into this wonderfully rich culture, and there I found a peace with just being one of the group. As I said it is one of my most prized gifts because it gives me the ability to be a part of this community. An understanding of black culture and things like code-switching presented the opportunity to move in the black community with comfort, knowing I would be accepted. If I didn't have this experience and knowledge, walking comfortably in the black community would be difficult, and acceptance into the black community would be nearly impossible.

Action Items for Families
1. Continue to search for ways to connect your child to his or her culture. Are there members of the birth family that can assist in this area?
2. Understand you need mentors as well as your children, someone who can help your family understand a culture that you have no history with. Many pause at the idea of friending someone simply because he or she is black. We don't pause when we approach the accountant we know to get her tax advice. Why is this any different? *Remember!* You are one contact away from changing your family's life for the better.

GETTING IT RIGHT

"Undercover" is my favorite chapter in the book. This is the chapter where I get the game-winning hit in baseball. *Every* time I read it I cry. "Decisions," the chapter on my running career and the state cross-country meet, is my second-favorite chapter. Every time I read this chapter I cry. I cry for the same reasons in both chapters. I cry for the little boy I was. I cry because I'm happy that the little boy got it right. I cry because I'm happy for the success the little boy achieved. I missed that lesson when these events happened.

No matter how much crying I do, it never washes away the adoption residue. The self-worth issues I have always struggled with and still struggle with don't rinse off. On those two Saturdays, I got it right, and even the meanest of coaches or most ill-timed of injuries couldn't take that away from me. For one Saturday I got to be a hero, and for the other I got to perform well above what was expected, and it feels so good to reread and relive those stories.

One sad realization I have come to is that when I was running and enjoying the attention of being a talented athlete, there was a war raging on in my head. The messages and whispers inside my head that said I wasn't worthy shouted down the successes I had, and I never truly understood just how talented I was until decades later. The battle in my head robbed me of so much joy.

As a parent of a transracial adoptee, one of your jobs is to help balance the scales. Many adoptees struggle with the same issues that I do, and the world does a great job of convincing us that we don't matter. As a parent, you have to balance the messages that come into your child's head. Take the time to build him or her up every chance you get. Give your child opportunities to get it right, and appreciate the talents and successes your child experiences.

Action Items for Families
1. Sit and read "Undercover" with your adoptees. Share with them why this always makes me cry. Ask them what they think they are good at, and point out to them the things that make them unique. Make a point to tell them they are gifted in something. Help quiet the whispers that try to tell them they aren't worthy.

STEREOTYPES AND RACIAL IDENTITY

There was something about black culture in the seventies and especially the eighties that made it heroic. The rap and hip-hop culture had invaded Detroit, and I clung to it as if it held life's breath. The images of blacks may not have been the most positive, but we were finally present and accounted for. Most people don't realize that black artists weren't on MTV until the eighties. It was big news when Michael Jackson's videos got regular play. So positive or not, the fact that blacks were being included was a huge deal.

My experience was such an atypical experience. I had friends both black and white who joined me in celebrating who I was and what my culture was, which just helped feed and fertilize the racial identity that was planted on Whitcomb Street.

My struggle for identity was awkward at times, and I didn't understand the bigger picture of how those around me would interpret me. My parents understood it more than I did, but I think they also wanted to give me space to explore who I was becoming.

During my high school years, as I was trying on my evolving identity, I wore a large black leather hat that looked like a leather version of Zorro's. I accessorized with black leather driving gloves and a black leather jacket. I was literally wearing what I thought was black. It was very "in" at the time, and when I wore it I felt like I was five feet ten, a half a foot taller than I was.

One fall evening, I was headed out to meet some of my friends, all geared up. We were going to go downtown. As I said good-bye to my mother, she paused and very gently said, "Do you think you should wear that going downtown?" The teenager in me didn't pay attention to her gentle warning, and I left without changing a stitch.

I understand now this was my mother's way of cautioning me. She knew how a young black teenager dressed in black leather would be perceived, and she was trying to nudge me to change outfits. I didn't understand the world beyond my teenage mind. I didn't understand that dressing like that could have brought on trouble that I didn't want from other teenagers or law enforcement. Fortunately, my trip downtown was uneventful.

Parents, there is a balance you have to find between allowing your children to explore who they are and making sure they are safe. You must have the tough conversations with your children about how some may perceive them.

Action Item for families

1. Have a conversation about stereotypes. Explain what they are, and then come up with some known stereotypes that apply to your children. Share with them the story of me, my Zorro outfit, and my mother's word of caution. Discuss what my mother was trying to do and why that is necessary. Explain perception versus reality.

ADVOCATING FOR YOUR CHILD

While I was speaking in Dayton a few years ago to a group of transracial parents, a white mother of a young black girl shared with group that recently her daughter had been reprimanded at school. Her daughter was the only child of color in the classroom, and with the new school year and a new teacher, her daughter appeared to be singled out by this one teacher more than she ever had been in previous years. As the mother relayed this story, she began with stating something just didn't feel right with the new teacher. As the story progressed, the mother began to explain away why her initial feelings were incorrect. Before I could even respond, the mother had convinced herself in retelling the story that her daughter, who could be "sassy" at times, had brought this on herself.

I explained to her that the uneasiness she had could very well be her intuition responding to the slights that come with racial bias. I explained that, as a parent of two black sons, I have the same struggle, but I owe it to my sons to consider that the slights and treatment they receive from others may have a racial component. I acknowledged that a larger part of me often wants to dismiss the slights as anything but racism or discrimination. Don't fall prey to this temptation. As parents, you must stay vigilant and have your wings ready to cover your children.

My parents had an unusual luxury a lot of transracial parents don't have today. When I was growing up, there was no such thing as being politically correct. So people felt justified in saying and doing whatever they felt. It made it easy to distinguish between allies and enemies. Today, so much is cloaked and disguised that it can be hard to discover. But a parent's intuition can unmask a lot. Trust what you are feeling, and don't dismiss it by arguing the intentions of the offender. Remember that you are your child's chief advocate and that intuition is telling you something isn't right for a reason. If your child is telling you over and over they feel slighted by a teacher, coach, or administrator, consider that there may be more to this than just a "sassy" child.

Part of the work I do now is working with school districts on diversity and inclusion. The struggle is getting the administrations to see the microaggressions and bias. My children had far more issues in school than I did, and because of their experiences and our frustrations and my work with schools, I was able to come to an understanding of what to do and not to do when an incident arises at school.

Action Item for Families

On the subject of advocating for you children of color, please keep this handy: don't get S.C.R.E.W.E.D. When an incident happens at school, do the following:

- **S:** Schedule an appointment with the administrator of the school. Only do so when you are calm. There is the urge to show up and kick down the doors when you feel your child has been wronged. Doing so will only get you labeled the irrational parent, and with that label comes no respect.
- **C:** Choose your battles wisely. Going up to the school every time your child is slighted again only erodes your reputation. If you are seen as a helicopter parent, you will be dismissed and ignored.
- **R:** Resist the urge to use the terms "racist" or "racism." Administrations aren't likely to see their staff or student body in this way, so again you will get dismissed as the overly dramatic parent. Learn what your school's hot buttons are, and use them to your advantage. Most schools have a policy on bullying. It is better to say you feel your child is being bullied. That gets more reaction. Remember you want action, and you have to learn what is the best way to get the quickest action.
- **E:** Expect the intentions argument: "Well, they didn't mean it like that…" You aren't there to argue intentions. You have a child who is hurting because of something that happened while he or she was in the care of the school. You want to know what is going to be done about it.
- **W:** Work for change but not at the expense of your child. You may be asked to work with the school to change things for the better, which is great, but don't lose sight of the fact that your child is hurting. That needs to be addressed before you will take on the district to change it.

- **E:** Experience this with your child. Let your child be involved, and keep him or her updated. This will teach your child how to advocate for himself or herself when you aren't around.
- **D:** Demand follow-up. Schools are great for talking about action right away, but then the emotion passes, and not much is done to prevent a harmful event from happening again. When you return home from the meeting, send an e-mail and copy yourself on it. In the e-mail, state your understanding of the meeting and when you expect follow-up. Word it in a way that requires a response, so you can document that the e-mail was received and responded to.

A NAME IS MORE THAN A NAME

My introduction to racial name-calling when I was seven or eight was actually a little behind schedule. Studies show that this behavior occurs typically between the ages of five and eight, and it is done specifically to hurt. As I stated, in my experience, being called "nigger" was the verbal atom bomb in a fight, and it was used purposely to hurt me.

My own sons were late bloomers as well. Six years ago, when my youngest was eight years old, he was called "nigger" during a recreational-league basketball game. He told his coach in the first quarter of the game, and his coach did nothing. My son was called "nigger" in the second quarter, and the refs were made aware, and they did nothing. My son was call "nigger" in the third quarter, and the other team's coach was made aware and did nothing. My son was called "nigger" in the fourth quarter, and he decided to make it stop. He pushed the boy who had called him a nigger the whole game, and my son was kicked out of the game. My son was crushed. Those verbal atom bombs shattered him each time they were dropped, and the adults involved did nothing to prevent my son from being assaulted.

Sadly this wasn't the last time my sons were called such names. Frankly, my boys were called "nigger" more than I ever was growing up. Let me repeat that: *my boys have been called "nigger" more than I ever was growing up!* It hasn't gone away, and I would argue in 2016 that everything is pointing to this name-calling getting worse before it gets better.

Last year my son played in the same league. A fellow teammate called my son a nigger, and the coach took swift action. The young man was kicked off the team, and I was surprised at how my son handled it. He was not wounded when it happened this time, and he was not crushed. Sadly this is part of the maturation process for children of color, and as his father I was both saddened and proud that he had come to this stage in his development. He had come to the understanding that being called nigger is a part of life as a child of color. He had come to accept that this horrible behavior and treatment were normal. It is painful to admit, but I was relieved he had come to this level in his racial development.

Are you as parents of children of color prepared for the day when your children will be on the receiving end of racial name-calling? How will you handle it?

I wish someone had told me the word was coming. I wish someone had prepared me for the assault *before* it happened. I wish I had been included in the solution and outcome of such an incident after it occurred.

Action Items for Families

1. Now that you know that racial name-calling typically occurs between the ages of five and eight, what are you going to do to prepare your children for this, if it hasn't happened already? Read the chapter "My First and Last," and discuss with your children how I felt and why. Ask them how they would feel if they were me. Let them know this type of behavior is not acceptable and that if it occurs, they are to let you know right away.

2. Rent or buy season four of the TV series *Parenthood*, and watch the episode entitled "The Talk." In this episode a black mother has a conversation with her biracial son about the word "nigger." She does a wonderful job explaining the word and talking to her son. Watch it with your child and discuss it.

WHAT TO DO WHEN PULLED OVER OR STOPPED BY THE POLICE

Families have requested this advice from me more than any other over the last few years. In black families, it is a conversation that is had with all kids. A good friend of mine who is the son of a Detroit police officer explained to me that his mother, the officer, gave him very clear instructions as to what to do when he was pulled over or interacted with police. I never got the instructions as a child, and I was fortunate that it never cost me too much.

When I explain to white parents raising children of color that there are different rules for these children, this topic is often met with frustration—frustration that their children have a different set of rules. My response to the frustration is to simply explain that if I have to follow a few extra rules to keep myself and my kids safe, I do it gladly.

These rules apply when you are pulled over in a car, whether you are driving or not, and they apply if you are stopped by the police. The number-one rule above all else is that your children must do whatever they have to come home to you.

Action Items for Families
1. Teach and review the following rules with your children well before they are of driving age.
2. Model this behavior when you are in the car with them and you are pulled over.

The Rules
1) Turn off the car, and turn off the radio.
2) Roll down all windows. Part of your job is to put the officer at ease. If he or she can see into the vehicle, that shows there is less of a threat to him or her.
3) If it's night, turn on the dome light to illuminate the inside of the vehicle.
4) Put your hands on the steering wheel with fingers spread apart, so the officer can see you have nothing in your hands.

5) Ask for permission to move, especially when reaching across the car.

6) Always answer, "Yes, sir," or, "No, sir."

7) Make a HOME kit for the dashboard.

The HOME Kit Instructions

1) Buy a cheap luggage tag.

2) Buy some Velcro squares.

3) Make a copy of license and registration.

4) Put this copy in the luggage tag.

5) Velcro the luggage tag to the dashboard.

6) Print a label and put this label on the luggage tag:

H. Honor and be humble.

O. Obey all commands.

M. Move slowly and with permission.

E. Easy does it. Breathe and stay calm.

This is so your child will remember what to do and that he or she must do whatever it takes to come home. Make sure your child understands this: Now is not the time to argue the legitimacy of the traffic stop. Just come home. You can argue those things later.

ENJOY YOUR FAMILY

I remember, when we all gathered for my father's funeral, being in the kitchen of my mom's house. I was having a conversation with my black brother-in-law about which soul foods I would and would not eat. He tried to convince me I should put slimy fried okra in my mouth. He failed.

In the living room, two of my sisters-in-laws, one from my brother's first marriage, were having a conversation in Chinese. My Japanese sister-in-law from my brother's second marriage, was having a conversation in Japanese with my niece and nephew. My mother and sister were having a conversation in English. I stood in awe of the truly multicultural family that was under one roof. This was the amazing result of a decision my parents made over forty-five years ago. We still have our struggles, but when I step back and look at it, we are an amazing family.

In your purposeful life, don't forget to take time to realize how amazing your family is because of *everyone* who is a part of it.

Action Items for Families
1. Go enjoy your wonderfully unique family.
2. Be wonderfully purposeful.
3. Raise wonderful-beyond-measure children.

Made in the
USA
Middletown, DE